10.04

L E G A L

B R E A K D O W N

40 WAYS TO FIX OUR LEGAL SYSTEM

NOLO PRESS • 950 PARKER STREET • BERKELEY, CA 94710

Printing History

FIRST EDITION

First Printing	November 1990
Second Printing	October 1991

■ Nolo books are available at special discounts for bulk purchases for sales promotions, premiums and fund-raising. For details contact: Special Sales Director, Nolo Press, 950 Parker Street, Berkeley, CA 94710.

Legal breakdown : 40 ways to fix our legal system / by Stephen Elias

  ... [et al.].

     p. cm.

  ISBN 0-87337-136-4 : $8.95

  1. Justice, Administration of--United States. 2. Courts--United States. I. Elias, Stephen.

KF8700.L38 1990

347.73'1--dc20   90-22317

[347.3071]   CIP

Contents

About the Authors, Editors and Publisher

Nolo Press was founded in 1971 with the publication of a book called *How to Do Your Own Divorce in California*. Twenty years later, we publish 80 books—nearly half for a national audience—to show people how to do diverse legal tasks such as filing for bankruptcy, obtaining a patent and drafting a will. We also produce self-help law software, audio tapes and videos, and publish a quarterly newspaper, the *Nolo News*.

Nolo's goal is to make law more accessible and fair for all. To this end, we actively support legislation aimed at breaking the legal profession's strangle hold on the legal system and encourage non-lawyers to take responsibility for their own legal concerns.

Nolo has a staff of about a dozen legal writers and editors. With outside authors, this group creates Nolo's new self-help law books and computer programs and keeps our ever-increasing list of old ones up to date. *Legal Breakdown* has been a pleasant change for us. Instead of a "how-to" book about a specific subject, such as adoption, incorporation or debt problems, its focus on improving the legal system has given us the opportunity to gather an eclectic mix of ideas and weave them into 40 specific proposals.

Nolo editors Steve Elias, Mary Randolph, Barbara Kate Repa and Ralph Warner formed Nolo's core editorial and writing group for the *Legal Breakdown* project. David Brown, Denis Clifford, Lisa Goldoftas, Tony Mancuso, Kate McGrath and Marcia Stewart also made writing contributions. Catherine Jermany, Robin Leonard and Albin Renauer contributed many creative suggestions.

The Legal Breakdown

The American civil legal system is slow, expensive and inaccessible. Too often, it's also unjust and corrupt. The core cause of this breakdown is that lawyers have been allowed to shape the legal system to serve their own purposes instead of the public's.

More than 100 million people who have legal problems can't afford to hire lawyers, according to the American Bar Association. Even if people are willing to handle routine legal procedures themselves, it is often impossible for them to get the most rudimentary information or guidance.

Consider a few symptoms of a legal system organized to deny the American public access to law:

- Laws are hard to find and even harder to understand.
- Lawyers' hourly fees run about ten times the average person's hourly wage.
- Court clerks and judges are generally hostile to self-help efforts; easy-to-use forms and procedures are rare.
- Many legal procedures, from transferring a house to probating an estate, are unnecessary and serve only to generate income for lawyers.
- Non-lawyers who try to compete with lawyers by providing high quality, low-cost legal form preparation services are labeled criminals.

Even worse is the larger failure of the legal system: It often hurts those who turn to it for help. No matter where you look—divorce, auto accidents, medical malpractice or probate—the civil legal system, which is supposed to fairly resolve disputes, routinely and needlessly produces more harm.

For example, our tort system, which requires an injured person to prove someone else was at fault, fails to compensate tens of thousands of seriously injured victims of auto accidents and medical malpractice while it overcompensates a few. A no-fault approach, which would fairly compensate all injured victims, would be more efficient and more just. But the present system is so astoundingly profitable for trial lawyers that they pour money into campaign contributions and lobbying efforts to thwart reform efforts.

Divorce is even worse, as anyone who has lived through it can attest. Instead of a process that helps people separate with dignity, lawyers preside over a needlessly contentious system which all too often turns peoples' pain into lawyers' billable hours.

In this book we make forty suggestions to make the American legal system fairer, faster, cheaper and more accessible. Each of these essays offers a practical reform—a new way of looking at some antiquated or wrong-headed aspect of the legal system. We focus tightly on how laws, courts, legal procedures and judges deny Americans reasonable access. We intentionally bypass the role of the legal system in perpetuating larger societal wrongs such as sexual and racial inequality and the miserable consequences of gross economic inequality.

These ideas come largely from Nolo Press's twenty years of experience as a pioneer in providing non-lawyers with self-help materials and from what we've heard from those who have been dealt unfair hands by the civil legal system. We make no claim that all of the thoughts in *Legal Breakdown* are original; we have consciously drawn on the ideas of a generation of legal reformers. Neither do we present these proposals as the final word on how to humanize our legal system. Our purpose is to open debate and encourage others to add their voices. We present these suggestions with a heathy dollop of optimism. Public alarm and outrage at the miserable muddle of our once-proud system of law and justice raises honest hope for reform.

In some countries, the course of the courts is so tedious, and the expense so high, that the remedy, Justice, is worse than injustice, the disease.

—Benjamin Franklin

1 Take Simple Actions Out of Court

Each day, tens of thousands of "legal" tasks, including uncontested name changes, adoptions, divorces and probates, are presented to American judges. This is as needless as it is costly. Courts are a miserable place to handle routine paperwork.

Courts are designed to handle adversarial proceedings, where lawyers argue for each side and a great deal of time and money are spent concocting and debating legal theories. Over centuries, elaborate rules on filing and pleading have evolved—many for reasons that no longer make sense. But even granting that some of this formality may be important to protect people's rights during a full-blown trial, it makes court an inefficient place for handling simple, uncontested issues such as adoptions or probates. Add to this the fact that busy judges rarely have time to properly evaluate uncontested cases, and it's easy to see that the judge's signature adds nothing but ink.

Relegating uncontested matters to the courts is unnecessary and inefficient for several other reasons:

■ Many personal decisions don't need ratification by a judge. No one gets a judge's seal of approval before having children or remarrying. Similarly, the common practice of a judge formally approving a stepparent adoption—especially when a social services agency has already investigated and approved it—serves no useful purpose.

■ Taking up court time for uncontested matters contributes mightily to the courts' increasingly huge backlog of contested cases.

■ Courts are complicated and intimidating. Even though the paperwork necessary to accomplish an uncontested task may be simple, the fact that an appearance before a judge is involved automatically sends many people trundling off to a lawyer. The unfortunate result is that they pay $150 an hour for a lawyer's secretary or paralegal to fill in forms that are often no more complicated than an application for a driver's license.

WHAT TO DO

Uncontested matters—adoptions, conservatorships, divorces, probates, guardianships and others—should be removed from court entirely. A few of these court procedures, such as the processes necessary to change one's name or probate an estate, should simply be abolished.

Other matters, such as divorce and adoption, should be taken out of court and handled by administrative agencies that have the expertise to process them efficiently and knowledgeably. The government would still be able to keep important records and look out for the interests of the people involved, but the expense and delay that come with any court process would be avoided.

A good system of administrative registration and regulation should have reasonable filing fees. All paperwork would be submitted on fill-in-the-blanks forms provided by the agency. The agency should also provide clear instructions and, where necessary, help for confused filers.

A couple who wanted an uncontested divorce, for example, could just fill out the necessary paperwork and mail or take it to the agency. The agency staff could be available to help them complete and file the forms, all without a lawyer. When the divorce was approved—a routine matter unless a problem was discovered—the divorce de-

cree could be mailed back to the former spouses.

To protect people who should have a voice in the outcome of some types of actions, all those who might reasonably be expected to have an interest should be identified when the first papers are filed.

In rare instances, when someone wanted to object—for example, if someone wanted to challenge a stepparent adoption—he or she could do so and have the case transferred to a court, where a full hearing could take place.

In addition to being more efficient, a streamlined and accessible system like this would cumulatively save people huge amounts in lawyer fees. And because running an agency is far cheaper than running a court, taxpayers would save lots of money as well.

 HISTORICAL BRIEF

Norman civil courts required plaintiff and defendant to plead their own cases, but on rare occasions, granted only by royal writ, substitutes could appear. At these times, an attorney, or *responsalis,* represented the absent party. Inevitably, substitution became more and more common and soon, despite a great deal of resistance, attorneys became a fixture. These attorneys were not officers of the court or a recognized profession, but as early as the twelfth century, certain names began to show up suspiciously often. By the thirteenth century, the idea that people with disputes had direct access to the tribunals established to resolve them was all over. Lawyers had come to dominate the courts.

The headaches started immediately. In 1240, the Abbott of Ramsey declared that none of his tenants was to bring a pleader into his courts to impede or delay justice. A revealing pronouncement of 1275 threatened imprisonment for the attorney guilty of collusive or deceitful practice. In a record of 1280, the mayor and aldermen of London lamented the ignorance and ill manners of the lawyers who practiced in the civic courts, and promised suspension for any who took money with both hands or reviled an antagonist.

From *Devil's Advocates: The Unnatural History of Lawyers* by Andrew Roth and Jonathan Roth (Nolo Press).

It is revolting to have no better reason for a rule of law than that so it was laid down in the time of Henry IV.
—Justice Oliver Wendell Holmes, Jr.

2   Abolish Probate

The probate system—the court-supervised process by which a deceased person's property is distributed—is in most cases a lengthy and expensive waste of time. As millions of Americans learn when the will of a family member or friend is probated, the system rarely benefits anyone but lawyers.

Probate is a relic—a holdover that traces its roots to feudal law. No other country still has a lawyer-ridden probate system like ours. Even England, the source of our probate law, eliminated its probate court system in the 1920s.

But in this country, unless you make other arrangements during your life, the probate court will oversee distribution of your property after you die. The process is an elaborate, needless legal dance, full of papers to be filed, notices to be served and published, inventories, appraisals and court hearings. Eventually—usually, after more than a year—the court orders the property to be turned over to the beneficiaries.

But before beneficiaries get a thing, hefty lawyers' fees are deducted. In a typical probate, lawyers' fees consume five to seven percent of the property—$25,000 to $35,000 of a $500,000 estate. A recent study by the American Association of Retired Persons estimated that American lawyers receive $1.5 billion a year in probate fees.

Usually, the lawyer's fee bears no relation to the work actually done; most lawyers charge a percentage of the value of the estate. Some states still have such percentage fees enshrined in statutes; unsuspecting clients don't know that they're legally entitled to negotiate a lower fee. And because probate is primarily a matter of tedious paperwork, many lawyers turn the actual work over to paralegals.

Probate's defenders are, unsurprisingly, mostly lawyers. They assert that the system protects beneficiaries by making sure they receive property left to them and protects creditors by making sure they are paid from the estate.

The reality is that very few estates need these alleged benefits. Most people use a will to leave their property to a few loved ones and to name a trusted friend or family member to supervise distribution. And most people do not have serious debt problems when they die. What debts remain can simply be paid from the property they leave. For the rare estate with tangled finances or complex legal claims, court supervision can be valuable. But that's no reason to require all wills to go through probate.

Because probate has become widely discredited and mistrusted, a substantial industry has grown up to show people how to avoid it. There are dozens of ways to leave property without having it go through probate, including holding property in joint tenancy, putting money in pay-on-death savings accounts and buying life insurance. Millions have used one of the most popular avoidance methods, a living trust. With a living trust, property is usually transferred to beneficiaries within a few days or weeks after its owner's death. No court proceeding of any kind is required.

So, in one sense, there is already a solution to the probate mess. People have voted with their feet—they've walked away from the system. But this isn't a satisfying solution, of course. Less financially sophisticated people who don't plan ahead to avoid probate must not be victimized.

WHAT TO DO

A few states, including Wisconsin and Maryland, have made efforts toward simplifying probate procedures. They have streamlined procedures and encourage people to handle probate without a lawyer. California and some other states have created fill-in-the-blank forms for probate paperwork and have simplified procedures for transferring small amounts of property or property that is left to a surviving spouse.

These reforms, however, don't go nearly far enough. The entire probate system should be abolished. The people who inherit property should be allowed to transfer its ownership without court supervision, bypassing the current inefficient and costly probate system. In most cases, putting inherited property into the name of the new owner is a simple process, requiring only a small amount of paperwork.

A will should become enmeshed in court proceedings only if someone challenges its validity. Because such challenges are quite rare, most people would never have to face the stress and expense of needless court proceedings.

THE HIGH COST OF DYING

Marilyn Monroe's estate offers an extreme example of how outrageous probate fees can be. She died in debt in 1962, but over the next 18 years, her estate received income, mostly from movie royalties, in excess of $1,600,000.

When Monroe's estate was settled in 1980, her executor announced that debts of $372,136 had been paid, and $101,229 was left as the final assets of the estate for distribution to inheritors.

Well over a million dollars of Monroe's estate was consumed by probate fees.

RESOURCES

HALT, an organization of Americans for legal reform, has pushed for probate reform in states across the country and can provide information on efforts in your state. Write to HALT at 1319 F Street, NW, Washington DC 20004.

The American Association of Retired Persons study on the probate system is available from AARP, 1909 K Street, NW, Washington, DC 20049. It also publishes a booklet called "A Consumer's Guide to Probate," which gives an overview of the probate process.

3 Strengthen Lemon Laws

An estimated 100,000 vehicles (1% of new cars coming off assembly lines each year) are seriously defective. Buyers end up taking these cars to and from the shop month after month after month. Although legislatures have tried to help people who end up with these lemons, too many purchasers still end up with little or no meaningful redress.

Nearly all states have some type of "lemon law" to protect buyers of new cars with serious problems that can't be fixed. Here's how the typical lemon law works. The problem must occur within one year or the car's warranty period, whichever comes sooner. A consumer who has a lemon is entitled to an arbitration hearing, where a panel hears both sides of the dispute. In most states, the manufacturer must follow the panel's decision if it recommends refunding the purchase price or replacing the vehicle. The buyer may be able to go to court if he or she isn't satisfied with the panel's decision.

Unfortunately, most lemon laws are seriously flawed. Even though arbitration hearings are free and designed to take place without a lawyer, car manufacturers are at a distinct advantage because they are more experienced at arbitration procedures than the typical consumer. And several of the larger auto companies establish and administer their own arbitration panels which tend to be pro-manufacturer. In addition, some panels base their decisions only on written submissions from each party—which doesn't allow the car owner to respond to the manufacturer's side of the story.

Second, the process takes too long. Dealers usually get three or four attempts to fix a particular defect (or approximately 30 days in the shop) before a buyer can pursue lemon law remedies. After the arbitration hearing, which requires considerable preparation time, up to 60 days may elapse before a decision is made. And then more time will pass if the car buyer doesn't like the ruling and chooses to continue the fight in court.

Third, the laws are vague. The typical legal definition of a lemon is a "substantial defect which impairs the car's use, value or safety." Many defects don't qualify. With rare exceptions, used cars are not covered by lemon laws at all.

Fourth, the consumer unfairly bears the burden of proving that a car is a lemon. For example, the buyer may need to show that the car's market value is severely reduced because of a defect. The consumer must also show that he or she jumped through all the hoops required to get a refund or replacement. If a hoop is missed—such as failing to notify the manufacturer in writing of the defect—the case and work may be out the window.

Fifth, many car buyers' costs (including "consequential" damages such as renting a car while the lemon was in the shop), are not paid even if the buyer wins in arbitration.

WHAT TO DO

Lemon laws could easily be improved if states would:

■ Develop better, clearer criteria for what constitutes a lemon. The approach in Massachusetts, where a car is legally a lemon if it's in the shop for 15 business days for either one major problem or a combination of less serious defects, should be adopted nationwide.

■ Let consumers with lemons go straight to arbitration programs run by the state or by an independent consumer agency, as in New York, rather than first submitting to a manufacturer's program.

■ Allow oral arbitration hearings, and give the car buyer the right to receive a copy of all papers the manufacturer presents so there are no surprises at the hearing.

■ Require manufacturers to decide cases within 40 days and allow them to reimburse consumers for consequential damages.

■ Expand lemon law coverage to used cars, at least for major systems such as brakes, power train and engine.

■ Produce brochures on lemon laws and consumer rights for dealers to give new car buyers at the time of purchase. These booklets should explain what consumers need to document their case before arbitration and include a sample step-by-step guide to the arbitration process.

RESOURCES

Lemon Book (Ralph Nader, Clarence Ditlow and Center for Auto Safety, 1990). An excellent book on buying and owning a new car, including how to avoid buying a lemon, legal rights and remedies, and state-by-state lemon laws.

To find out about your state's lemon law and how to use it, contact your state's Attorney General's Office or consumer protection agency.

For information on safety problems with your particular car's make and model contact:

National Highway Traffic Safety Administration
400 7th Street, SW, Washington DC 20590
(800) 424-9393

Center for Auto Safety
2001 S Street, NW, Washington DC 20009
(202) 328-7700

4 Simplify Legal Paperwork

Courts require documents to be written new for each legal procedure, laid out according to arbitrary rules and typed on a kind of numbered paper used nowhere else. This complexity both intimidates people who go to court without a lawyer and wastes the time of lawyers and courts.

Drafting legal documents has been a lucrative skill among lawyers for centuries. From the start, American courts were saddled with a cumbersome array of documents. Their models were the English courts of the time, which even then were notorious for requiring intricate documents, written in Latin.

Trumped-up complexity, of course, has always been the lifeblood of lawyers. Mastering the elaborate paperwork of the legal system is one of their most salable skills. Anyone who wants access to the courts must hire a lawyer who knows how to draw up papers that will open the courtroom door.

Not until very recently—within the last 20 years—did a few courts abandon the idea of documents crafted for each situation. These courts realized that they could simplify their own work considerably by using standardized, fill-in-the-blanks forms. Lawyers who completed well-designed forms were more likely to supply the data the court needed than those who prepared old style pleadings.

Even lawyers who at first resisted quickly found standardized forms to be a bonanza. Forms made many of their tasks much simpler—and so easier to delegate to secretaries and paralegals.

One unintended consequence of easy-to-use forms is a huge increase in the number of people who handle their own legal problems. It's no coincidence that California, which pioneered the use of standardized forms, leads the country in court cases filed without lawyers.

A couple who wants to get an uncontested divorce, for example, wouldn't know how to write a legal request for one. But they can fill out a simple form that asks questions about their income, property and children. It is comparable to the difference between filling out an income tax return and writing a narrative to explain your income, deductions and tax due. Of course, the IRS, which is designed to get quick results, has had forms for generations.

Standardized paperwork also encourages people to be less dependent on lawyers and instead get help from self-help materials and legal typing services. Someone who doesn't want to go it alone can use a self-help book that contains tear-out forms and instructions. Or, for more help, a typing service staffed by non-lawyers—often, former legal secretaries or paralegals—will know how to prepare and file the forms correctly.

Unfortunately, standardized forms are still the rare exception to the rule. Few courts offer them, and in most places they are available only for a few matters, such as temporary restraining orders. And even courts that have forms pass them out without instructions, leaving people to fend for themselves.

WHAT TO DO

Standardized forms should be available for most routine legal matters: requesting or opposing eviction, adoption, child support, filing a personal injury lawsuit, probate and divorce are obvious ones.

All standardized forms should come with clear, line-by-line instructions. This is a truly radical notion in a system based on hiding the smallest instruction. It shouldn't be. Comprehensive instructions on how, where and when to file legal documents would not only make the task easier for those who file, it would free up court personnel to deal more efficiently with the business of the courts. People should also be able to get help from court clerks, over the phone and in person.

WHERE THINGS WENT WRONG...

Efforts at simplifying legal paperwork and procedure have proceeded in fits and starts for the entire history of this country. The colonists allowed the use of English instead of Latin, for example, but complexities soon crept in. Before 1700, lawyers—who had originally been barred in many colonies—had already imported writs of *scire facias*, lawsuits for *trespass de bonis asportatis* and other similarly mysterious creatures. Judges took on kingly airs, throwing out cases if the papers misspelled a name, gave the defendant's occupation incorrectly or made other trivial errors.

As the legal profession grew in power during the 18th and early 19th century, the relatively simple colonial procedures were gradually submerged under a tide of complexity. For their inspiration, lawyers looked back (some would say backwards) to the intricate English system of pleading.

In the mid-1800s, the pendulum swung back in a more democratic direction. People no longer needed law licenses to appear in court in many states, and there were a number of efforts to make law more understandable. The most revolutionary breakthrough in procedure came when a New York commission proposed a radically simplified system of pleading. The idea was to make the paperwork straightforward enough so that the average person could go to court without a lawyer. Many lawyers, of course—the same folks who brought us *trespass de bonis asportatis*—fought the idea. But it caught on, especially in the newer western states.

Further reform efforts have been stalled for most of this century. Bar associations consolidated their hold on the legal system, and there have been few crusaders to attack the red tape of the courts. But as public outrage again grows at a system that needlessly freezes out all but lawyers, that may change.

*Poor people have access to the courts
in the same sense that the Christians had
access to the lions when they were
dragged into a Roman arena.*

—Judge Earl Johnson, Jr.

5 Make the Courthouse User-Friendly

People have the right to represent themselves in court without a lawyer. But if they try, they often find that courthouses and court procedures are needlessly hard to navigate. To make matters worse, a person without a lawyer usually gets no help from clerks, judges and other courthouse personnel.

Most matters that go before a judge are unopposed; all that's needed for success is the right paperwork. Anyone with enough information should be able to go it alone, without hiring a lawyer. But from beginning to end, the legal system makes it hard—sometimes impossibly hard—for intelligent and reasonable people to accomplish what should be routine legal tasks.

It's obvious, from the moment you walk in, that courthouses aren't designed for anyone but lawyers. Unlike most government facilities, there's rarely a central information desk or window. The kind of informative pamphlets typically found in a Social Security or IRS office are absent. Often there are special lounges, work areas and phones for lawyers, but benches and pay phones for everyone else.

Court personnel who could easily guide self-helpers through the labyrinth are often unhelpful and sometimes downright hostile. Many clerks are instructed by their superiors not to divulge even the most straightforward

information—for example, how to complete a certain blank of a fill-in-the-blanks form. They are told simply to advise people with questions to get a lawyer.

Even finding the right courtroom can be exhausting. In many courthouses, hundreds of litigants and lawyers must crowd into a room every morning while a judge or clerk reads off courtroom assignments with the speed of an auctioneer. Typically, ten or more court hearings are scheduled for the same time while waiting to be called, lawyers who have other business in the courthouse can use their time, but people who represent themselves must cool their heels.

This lack of respect for the public is also reflected in courtroom procedures. People without lawyers are sometimes heard last, to accommodate the busy lawyers representing clients. The judge is likely to adopt the patronizing attitude some adults use around children. Someone who hesitates or makes a small mistake, even an easily corrected one, may be accused of clogging the court's calendar and told to get a lawyer. In complicated cases, the problem is even worse, because bias against someone without a lawyer may cloud a judge's judgment about the merits of the case.

Most court clerks, lawyers and judges, for whom the current system is familiar and comfortable, don't even see the many barriers that deny non-lawyers equal access to the legal system. Without thinking much about it, they accept as legitimate the idea that to enter the judicial system, citizens must pay a gatekeeper—a lawyer.

WHAT TO DO

Courts must be examined from top to bottom with an eye to eliminating this pervasive and essentially anti-democratic bias. Like other complicated bureaucracies, every courthouse should have employees whose only job is to help people navigate the courts.

An "access catalog," designed like a college course catalog, should describe what the court can do for people. It should spell out how much a procedure costs, how long it takes and where to find more information.

Courts should also distribute materials to help people with every step of the process. Preprinted forms should come with complete instructions. Pamphlets, books, recorded telephone messages that answer common questions and videotapes that show how the court process works should all be readily available at the courthouse. Courts should encourage filing documents by mail to cut down on repeat trips to the courthouse.

To ensure accountability, a non-lawyer board of directors could monitor a courthouse's treatment of the public. Such a board could also deal with complaints from the public.

In the final analysis, the human element may be the most important. Judges and clerks should treat self-helpers with courtesy and respect. They should be reminded that the system was originally intended to serve the public (not lawyers).

Divorce involves not only facts but feelings, and we're not able to legislate feelings.

—Ann L. Milne
Divorce mediator

6 Mediate Child Custody and Support Disputes

Few events in modern life produce more bitterness and hurt than child custody disputes, especially when children are young. Sadly, the American legal system does much to make these disagreements more miserable. Adversarial court procedures fan paranoia, encourage perjury and turn children into expendable pawns in an emotional battle.

Our legal system magnifies disputes over child custody, visitation and support by encouraging parents to fight them out in the hostile arena of a courtroom. Sometimes these battles last for years, or until money to pay the lawyers runs out, with each parent escalating the attack to meet or beat the other.

Fortunately, there is a better approach: mediation. Styles of mediation vary somewhat, but the main idea is that those faced with a dispute meet with a neutral third person and attempt to work out their own settlement. Unlike a court or arbitration proceeding, however, no decision is imposed on those who have the dispute. It's up to them to keep talking until they arrive at a compromise.

The mediator's role is to see that each person gets a fair chance to speak, ensure that neither is intimidated or overbearing, and perhaps to make suggestions to help the parties reach an agreement. Where state law sets guidelines for child support based on parental income, the mediator must also see that the agreement complies. In addition, most mediators reserve the right to veto any custody or support agreement that's clearly not in the long-term best interests of the children.

Despite the advantages of mediation, most people take custody disputes to court. Lawyers and judges trained to resolve disputes in an adversarial manner rarely voluntarily refer people to mediation. Private mediation programs run by psychologists, social workers, clergy or lawyers-turned-mediators have kept many people out of court. But private mediators typically charge from $75 to $200 per hour—out of reach for many people.

Mandatory court-sponsored programs that provide free mediation have been more successful in helping people who have disputes over child custody or support. The laws in California and a few other states require that people try free public mediation before fighting out their differences in court. The success rate of these programs is impressive: more than 80% of participants settle their disputes cooperatively.

But while mediation is vastly superior to a court fight, like any human system, it's not perfect.

First, to make intelligent decisions, each spouse needs good, detailed information about state laws on custody, support and visitation. Most mediators don't provide it.

Second, mediation raises the risk that a spouse with more business sense or psychological power will be able to coerce the other into agreeing to an inequitable result, such as accepting an inadequate amount of child support or allowing the other parent to unfairly dominate child-rearing decisions.

Third, if mediation is voluntary, a parent may pretend to mediate in good faith while following the instructions of a lawyer to let the mediation fail so the dispute can be taken into trial court.

WHAT TO DO

At the outset, separating parents should be given a thorough and easy-to-understand pamphlet explaining their legal rights and responsibilities toward their children. This should include guidelines on custody, visitation and support requirements.

All courts that handle divorce and custody disputes should have a free mediation program. Both married and unmarried couples who have disputes over children should be required to use this program, or a private mediator, before taking a contested custody or visitation dispute to court. If a mediating couple agrees on child support, custody and visitation, their agreement falls within state guidelines, and the mediator certifies that it is uncoerced and in the best interests of the children, it should take effect at once. If after a reasonable number of mediation sessions parents cannot agree, the dispute should be referred to court, along with the mediator's recommendation.

I seek the kind of verdict that makes the
angels sing and the cash registers ring.
—Melvin Belli
Personal injury lawyer

7 Regulate Contingency Fees

When handling car accident and other civil cases that promise big dollars, lawyers often take a large percentage of the amount recovered as their fees. Typically, these fees far exceed a reasonable rate for the services rendered or the risk taken. As a result, billions of dollars are diverted from clients directly into lawyers' bank accounts.

In lawsuits over personal injuries, lawyers customarily charge a "contingency fee" of 25% to 50% of the award or settlement. This means the lawyer gets paid very generously if the case is won, and nothing if it's lost.

In theory, this approach makes some sense. An injured person can get a lawyer's services without paying for them unless there is a successful result. Many people who can't afford to pay a lawyer's hourly rates can have their cases presented in court.

On closer examination, however, the contingency fee system amounts to little more than a get-rich-quick scheme for lawyers. Lawyers who win or favorably settle a contingency fee case almost always get paid far more than the time spent on the case justifies. Many personal injury attorneys earn hundreds of times more with contingency fees than they would if they charged by the hour.

Proof that contingency fee cases are outrageously profitable is found in a common practice of personal injury lawyers: They hand over one-third of the contingency fee to the lawyer who referred the case to them.

Personal injury lawyers justify these windfalls by arguing that they need large fees to balance out the cases where there is no recovery and they aren't paid for their work. But this argument is based on the false premise that when they take a case for no upfront fee, they also take a substantial risk of coming up empty-handed. The examples most often cited are complex expensive lawsuits against big corporations that poison the environment or their employees. But these cases are the exceptions. Most lawyers accept cases only if:

■ a favorable outcome is reasonably certain based on the facts and the law;

■ the damages suffered by the client will generate enough fees to make taking the case well worth the lawyer's while; and

■ there is an insurance company, city, corporation or other "deep pocket" defendant, which can afford either to buy its way out of the case by settling, or pay a judgment if the case goes to trial.

The harm caused to society by this scam is enormous. In addition to the billions of dollars siphoned off from injured victims, the possibility of huge contingency fee profits creates a kind of lawyer feeding frenzy. Lawyers bring lawsuits on flimsy grounds. They concoct massive class actions—lawsuits in which a small group of individuals sue on behalf of a larger group of similarly affected people—seeking hundreds of millions of dollars in damages. Some even assist clients in presenting perjured testimony. All these lawsuits in turn contribute to horrendous insurance rates for everyone.

WHAT TO DO

To correct contingency fee abuse, some kinds of lawsuits—for example, auto accident and medical malpractice cases—should be handled administratively on a no-fault basis. A lawyer should not be necessary, except perhaps to give limited legal advice or to help handle an appeal if an administrative claim is denied.

For other types of cases in which lawyers charge a contingency fee, the lawyer should be required to provide the client with a detailed written fee estimate. That estimate would be based on the anticipated number of hours the case will require from lawyers, paralegals and clerical staff. It would also include a ceiling on the fee if the hourly estimate proved inadequate.

To assess the chances of winning the case, the estimate would spell out:

- how clear the defendant's liability is;
- how difficult it will be to prove the extent of the injury; and
- how likely it is that a settlement or verdict will be collected from the defendant.

At the option of the client, the lawyer would either collect fees periodically based on the hours worked, or defer collection until the case was completed. For deferred payment cases, the lawyer could add interest to the fees that accrued during the case.

To keep lawyers honest, if the case is won or successfully settled, the lawyer would have to submit to the trial court the fee agreement and documentation of hours worked. This material would be part of the case file, accessible to the public.

If the case is lost, the lawyer would not get paid unless the risk in the case had been assessed to be over 50%, and the client agreed in writing, on the basis of the risk assessment, to be responsible for the fees regardless of the outcome. The lawyer's initial assessment could be reviewed by a fee arbitration panel at the client's request.

If the judge deemed the lawsuit to be in the public interest—a case against a toxic polluter or manufacturer of unsafe cars, for example—the judge would still have authority to decide whether attorneys should be paid by the defendant.

LIVING THE GOOD LIFE WITH CONTINGENCY FEES

A recent advertisement in *The Recorder*, a San Francisco legal newspaper, sported the headline "Millionaire Personal Injury Attorney Reveals Secrets." The ad touted a three-day seminar, generously promising to show other personal injury lawyers how to "unlock the door to incredible wealth in the personal injury field." The ad proclaimed that any lawyer can "handle 50-60 cases simultaneously, settle most cases within 60-90 days, [and] consistently get the highest settlements," all without increasing overhead.

The price? A flat $30,000. Anticipating that some might balk at this price, the ad offered a money-back guarantee. But given what attorneys can get under the contingency fee system if it is milked properly, a $30,000 seminar is probably a small price to pay.

A long habit of not thinking a thing wrong gives it a superficial appearance of being right, and raises at first a formidable outcry in defense of custom.

—Thomas Paine

8

Add Self-Help Court Clerks

Clerks are the gatekeepers of the courthouse. No legal action is possible until they put their stamp of approval on papers submitted to the court. Unfortunately, many clerks are indifferent, hostile or just too busy to help people who try to navigate the court system without lawyers.

Most court clerks refuse to answer simple procedural questions from people who need to file routine legal paperwork. Left on their own, without help, standardized forms or even rudimentary instructions, many people submit papers that these same clerks then reject for trivial errors. To add insult to injury, clerks commonly refuse to explain why papers are inadequate or to direct self-helpers to materials that could give them guidance. Because many self-helpers can't afford a lawyer, they are shut out of the legal system.

Clerks are under pressure from their supervisors—judges and court administrators—to deal quickly with people waiting in line. And they often defend their actions by arguing that assisting self-helpers is too time-consuming. They are partially right. It *is* time-consuming to help people who are unfamiliar with the legal labyrinth. But it's time well spent. Guaranteeing all people access to the legal system should be viewed as a priority, not an irksome chore.

Even if they had the time, say the clerks, giving self-helpers too much direction would put the clerks at risk of practicing law without a license—a criminal offense. So they hide

behind the familiar refrain of "We Are Not Authorized To Give Legal Advice." Their fear, however, is ungrounded. Few court clerks, if any, have ever been prosecuted for the unauthorized practice of law.

WHAT TO DO

In every court, clerks should be trained and directed to help everyone who seeks access to the courts, not just to those with law licenses.

To alleviate court clerks' fear of legal prosecution, statutes prohibiting the unauthorized practice of law could easily be rewritten to exempt clerks who dispense basic information to the public.

Certain clerks could be designated to provide assistance, in person and on the phone, to people who are handling a legal matter without a lawyer. The self-help clerks would be experts in court procedures and specially trained in dealing with the problems and pitfalls of legal paperwork. For example, they could tell a divorcing couple what forms they need to fill out for a simple, uncontested divorce, and could answer basic questions about how to fill them out. Ideally, the clerks could also distribute the forms, along with line-by-line instructions, published by the state.

They would not advise people about the law or help with the strategy for a lawsuit. If someone really needed legal advice, the clerks could recommend self-help materials or recommend getting an experienced lawyer's advice.

Because helping self-helpers through the system would be their sole task, the self-help clerks would not suffer the hurry-up angst that afflicts most clerks. When they took the time needed to explain a convoluted procedure, they would simply be doing their job—not slowing down the line for those who waited behind.

A good model for such a program is the system of small claims court legal advisors used in California. These advisors are available to help people who want to sue or are being sued in small claims court. They answer questions about filing procedures, preparing and presenting cases, and collecting judgments after cases have been decided.

The additional clerks' salaries could come from some of the document filing fees, which in many places are currently earmarked for such items as furniture for judges or books for lawyers. If that didn't cover all the expense, people needing assistance from self-help clerks could pay for it with slightly higher filing fees.

A DIFFERENT APPROACH IN WISCONSIN
COURT CLERKS WHO HELP SELF-HELPERS

In Madison, Wisconsin, those filing for probate after the death of a family member or friend have two choices. They can pay an attorney to do the job for them. Or they can handle it themselves in a specialized informal probate procedure that is part of the county court system. Those who go it alone have lots of help—forms, instructions and explanations from Probate Court Commissioner Daniel Breunig and his staff of three. They meet with those who file informally to discuss the probate procedure generally and to go over a checklist of forms that must be prepared and filed.

The forms are straightforward; to complete them, people need only fill in information such as names and addresses. Breunig says what people need the most is assurance that they have filled in the blanks properly.

When the simplified system went into effect in 1973, some predicted that as many as 90% of all probates filed in Wisconsin would be processed through the informal system. That never came to pass. Breunig says that only about one-third of the approximately 1,200 probates filed annually in Wisconsin are handled without lawyers.

Breunig says there are two reasons for this. "Traditionally, most people have believed the attorneys who have always told them, 'I'm this Superhero and I can do something you can't do,'" says Breunig. Another group of people, he says, would rather hire someone else to do their legwork and paperwork.

Those who file informally get almost unlimited help from Breunig and his staff along the way. "In two or three hours, we can steer someone through a conventional probate," Breunig says. "They save about $4,000 in attorneys' fees. But what they accomplish is even more amazing: They've conquered the grand mystique of the law."

9 Educate the Public About Law

Our schools provide next to no basic legal training. Most people learn about law only when faced with a crisis—such as a custody battle or dispute with a landlord. By then, it's often too late to gather enough information short of buying it from a lawyer.

Everyone agrees that law governs more and more aspects of our lives. Schools, especially, pay lofty lip service to the importance of an informed citizenry. Yet absurdly, the schools never teach the basic legal concepts that will inevitably affect their students' lives within a few years—the law of marriage, divorce, renting an apartment, employment and installment contracts.

It seems obvious that people should understand enough law to handle their own legal problems. But in addition, all sorts of societal institutions—the police, social services, landlords, the courts—will benefit if individuals are better able to cope with their legal needs. And people with a solid grounding in basic legal issues will have a much better idea of how and when they need more specialized legal help. So lawyers, too, have a positive interest in better basic legal education.

Adult legal education is another large under-met need. In most communities, there is no easy access to practical legal information. The few adult programs that do exist are typically administered, catch-as-catch-can, by bar associations whose financial self-interest is to enhance the status of attorneys as the principal source of all legal information. An example is the annual Law Day. Typically, it consists of lawyers making appearances on local television or at public meetings where they often answer consumers' legal questions by recommending that they hire lawyers. Other legal education programs, including workshops or brochures produced by well-meaning consumer protection agencies, tend to be irregular, publicized poorly and distributed to only a few people.

WHAT TO DO

Public legal education programs—beginning in the primary school classroom and continuing through adulthood—must be expanded. Educators, not practicing lawyers, need to be in charge. Most lawyers are so predisposed to seeing the law as their own property that it's impossible for them to grasp that legal information—like physics, beekeeping or Greek mythology—can be efficiently and widely taught.

States should require and fund law-related education as an organized and ongoing part of the public school curriculum, particularly high school. To accomplish this, teachers need materials and training on how to make everyday law come alive. It shouldn't be hard—students are curious about how all sorts of laws affect them and their families. Laws involving curfews, reproductive rights, even the right of school officials to search their lockers are just a few good examples.

A step in the right direction can be found in the "street law" programs now sponsored by 30 law schools throughout the country. In these programs, law students are given training and classroom materials and teach high school classes about practical legal problems, including housing and family law and how to resolve common disputes. The student teachers get academic credit, and many also come away with a better understanding of what people need to learn about the law.

For adults, community colleges, local school districts and college extension programs should offer more reasonably-priced courses on basic legal skills. In this area particularly, trained legal educators are sorely needed. The present practice of having these

courses taught by underemployed lawyers prospecting for clients must be stopped.

Finally, states should establish and publicize law-related education programs along with other consumer protection activities. As part of these programs, they should:

■ Publish and widely distribute consumer guides to basic state laws, from abortions to wills.

■ Establish legal clinics and tenants' rights groups to foster legal self-education and assistance.

■ Produce recorded legal messages callers can quickly dial up for practical information on common legal topics such as marriage, divorce and credit.

Public legal education programs can produce a great deal of information per dollar spent. Funding could come from using a small percentage of fines collected from traffic violations or littering—or from a portion of lawyers' bar association dues.

RESOURCES

School-Based Programs National Institute for Citizen Education in the Law (711 G Street, SE, Washington, DC 20003 [202] 546-6644) offers a wide variety of materials, training and technical assistance on law-related education in schools, adult education and other settings—including a comprehensive textbook, *Street Law: A Course in Practical Law* (West Publishing Co., St. Paul, MN 1986).

The American Bar Association's Special Committee on Youth Education for Citizenship (750 N. Lakeshore Drive, Chicago, IL 60611 312-988-5735) provides training materials and technical assistance for teachers, administrators and attorneys on law-related education in elementary through secondary schools.

Adult Programs The Community Legal Education Program at the Monterey College of Law (498 Pearl Street, Monterey, CA 93940 [408] 373-3301) offers free and low-cost legal self-help classes (landlord/tenant, small claims court, employment law) to the general public, taught by volunteer attorneys and judges.

A model legal hotline is Tel-Law, operated by the Riverside County Bar Association in Southern California (3612 7th Street, Riverside, CA 92501 [714] 682-5213). Ten offices throughout California offer free taped messages on hundreds of legal topics.

10 Eliminate Auto and Home Repair Rip-offs

Millions of consumers are victims each year of dishonest or incompetent auto repair shops and home repair contractors. Bad service not only wastes our time and money, but can directly endanger our safety. And the legal system has little success at preventing these problems or compensating ripped-off consumers.

Except for penalties for outright fraud and false advertising, state laws do not provide meaningful protection against bad auto or home repairs. This is true despite the existence of state agencies, financed by millions of our tax dollars, that oversee the repair industry. Here's what's wrong with the current system:

■ Few states certify the practical skills of auto mechanics or contractors.

■ Complaining to regulatory agencies is typically a waste of time. Too often, they have become the captives of their own industries. And too often, these industries use campaign contributions and other forms of influence-peddling to ensure that legislatures don't enact effective regulation.

■ It's usually impossible to find out which repair firms consistently do a lousy job. Some government agencies do accept complaints against individual auto and home repair firms for shoddy or incomplete work, but do not make them available to the public. Those complaints that are made public often first require some

legal violation—theft, fraud or failure to post a bond. Incompetence, however, is not against the law, so is usually not a matter of public record.

This means that it's not until after the fact that we can judge the proficiency of the people who work on our cars and homes. By that time, the consequences may be miserable (if the work is done so poorly that we have to spend time and money having it done over) or even disastrous (if brakes aren't fixed properly or inferior materials are used for home repair).

Almost as bad, if we get bad service, we have virtually no place to go for help short of filing a lawsuit. Even small claims court, assuming the dollar limit is high enough to cover the claim, is relatively time-consuming. And if you win, it still may be hard to collect the money on a small claims judgment.

WHAT TO DO

To legislate a better system, agencies controlled by the public should provide cost-effective regulation of home repair contractors and auto mechanics in the consumer interest. Here's how:

Register. People who do auto and home repair work should be required to register with the state so they can be located if a problem surfaces later.

Test and licenses. To protect the public against incompetence, states should require auto mechanics and contractors working on major home repair projects to pass practical tests demonstrating competence in the specific types of work they do. All auto and home repair firms should pay a yearly fee to the state to finance these programs.

Settle disputes out of court. States should establish low-cost, impartial programs to accept and mediate complaints against mechanics and contractors. Face-to-face discussions with a neutral third person—a mediator—to try to reach a compromise, should occur within one month after a complaint is filed.

When mediation is unsuccessful, states should require prompt binding arbitration—a process in which one or more independent experts makes a final decision based on the merits of the case. The arbitration process should include the testimony of independent experts competent to judge the quality of auto or home repair work in disputed cases. If a ruling favors a consumer, the repair company should be required to pay promptly, including the cost of arbitration, or do the job over, on pain of having its license suspended.

Disclose complaints. To help consumers make informed decisions, states should disclose the exact nature of past and current complaints filed against a specific auto repair shop or home repair firm and the status or resolution of each complaint.

Compensate rip-off victims. A repair firm that does shoddy or fraudulent work may be out of business by the time an arbitration award is made. If so, individuals who can no longer collect should do so from a consumer compensation fund. Part of the license fee charged contractors and mechanics should be used to raise the necessary money.

RESOURCES

Help in Choosing a Contractor The National Association of Home Builders (15th and M Streets, NW, Washington, DC 20005 [202] 822-0200) publishes a free brochure, *How To Choose a Remodeler Who's on the Level,* on how to select a home improvement contractor, protect yourself in a written contract and resolve disputes.

How to Complain *Consumer's Resource Handbook* (available free from the Consumer Information Center, Pueblo, CO 81009) provides general advice on how to file complaints against a business and choose auto repair and home remodeling services.

Compensation for Victims At least five states (Arizona, Connecticut, Hawaii, Maryland and Virginia) have established funds to reimburse consumers who are victims of dishonest or incompetent contractors. To find out more, contact your state's consumer protection office, listed in the government section of the phone book white pages.

11 Fairly Compensate Victims of Auto Accidents

The current system of trying to compensate victims of automobile accidents based on who was at fault is unjust, dishonest and slow. Lawyers and administrative fees consume well over half of every dollar that goes to victims. It's a system that works brilliantly for lawyers, but no one else.

In most states, an auto accident trial consists of a high-stakes battle to get a jury to pin blame on one person for an accident that occurred years earlier. The victim who is successful at this recovers big bucks, including payment for pain and suffering, routinely set at four or five times as much as the often-inflated cost of medical bills, rehabilitation and loss of pay. The victim who is unsuccessful at trial, even one who has traumatic injuries, receives little or nothing.

Cruel as this system is, it would be at least logically defensible if it accurately determined who was at fault and made them—or their insurance companies—pay. It doesn't. Given today's powerful vehicles and congested roads, it's extremely difficult to precisely determine fault—especially when an accident occurs at night, at freeway speed, or is triggered by the carelessness of a person who avoids the smash-up. For example, who pays when five cars crash while trying to avoid a driver who suddenly cuts across three lanes and then disappears down an exit ramp?

As difficult as it is to accurately determine fault a few minutes after an accident occurs, it's next to impossible three or four years later, at trial, when a jury is faced with witnesses who have been coached by lawyers. With lots of money hanging in the balance and lawyers getting a big percentage of whatever the victims are awarded, but nothing if they lose, there are many incentives for perjury.

The present system is also painfully slow. Victims must usually wait three or more anxious years before a case gets to court and they find out if they will be compensated.

Finally, trying to determine fault is a huge money-guzzling process. By the time you add up the legal fees of both injured victims and recalcitrant insurance companies, lawyers get over 50% of the total settlement dollar—billions of dollars that could be far better used to compensate injured victims and the families of the dead.

It's these easy-come fees that have blocked the way to a fairer, more humane compensation system. American trial lawyers have become the true pigs of the legal road, marshaling their formidable political power in state legislatures to retain the system which keeps them fat. They simply put politicians on their payroll through campaign contributions, speaking fees and the like.

WHAT TO DO

States should adopt true no-fault automobile insurance—a system that promptly compensates all motor vehicle accident victims for their actual monetary loss, regardless of who was at fault, but provides no payment for pain and suffering.

Under a good no-fault system, accident victims would file claims with a no-fault insurer much the way victims of workplace accidents currently apply for workers' compensation. Compensation would be available for property damages, medical costs, rehabilitation costs and loss of income. In addition, when a death or disabling injury occurred, a fair allowance should be paid to a surviving spouse, children and other dependents to cover living and education costs.

BEWARE OF WATERED-DOWN NO-FAULT

In the past twenty years, a number of states have passed so-called no-fault insurance laws that actually perpetuate the fault system. For example, they may restrict no-fault claims to a low amount, such as $10,000 for medical expenses. Bigger claims still go to court under fault rules. It's easy for lawyers, eyeing large settlements for pain and suffering, to inflate claims. and get a case out of the no-fault system and into court.

Still another way to water down no-fault laws is to limit coverage to certain types of injuries. Typically, more serious injuries, such as permanent disability or loss of a limb, are exempted. Again, this makes little sense, because it is precisely in these big dollar lawsuits that the present system produces the worst abuses.

A BETTER WAY

Recognizing that laws mandating true no-fault auto insurance are almost impossible to enact, Jeffrey O'Connell and Robert Joost have proposed giving motorists a choice between no-fault and conventional fault-based insurance.

If they choose a no-fault policy, they would give up the right to sue others based on who was at fault in an accident. In exchange, the premium would be cheaper. A motorist who chose no-fault insurance and then had an accident would be compensated up to the limits of the policy for medical costs, loss of wages and other direct economic losses. The victim would not be compensated for non-economic losses, such as pain and suffering. However, if the motorist bought a conventional policy, normal fault-based rules would apply. If this motorist were injured and could prove someone else was at fault, he or she would recover for pain and suffering as well as for direct economic losses.

For information on reforming our tort system generally, including an excellent chapter on no-fault automobile insurance, see *The Blame Game: Injuries, Insurance and Injustice,* by Jeffrey O'Connell and C. Brian Kelly (Lexington Books, 1987).

The average American judge, as everyone knows, is a mere rabbinical automaton, with no more give and take in his mind than you will find in the mind of a terrier watching a rathole.

—H.L. Mencken

12 Make Judges Disclose Bias

A biased judge can sway the outcome of a jury trial, and absolutely predetermine the result of a court trial. Amazingly, a judge's background, investments and mindset are seldom disclosed to the people involved in a case.

There is no problem more fundamental to the goal of a fair legal system than hidden judicial bias. In cases heard by judges alone—much more common than jury trials—a hidden bias is very likely to unfairly determine the result.

Even in jury trials, judges make dozens of decisions about the evidence presented by the parties and the tactics of the attorneys. They have the power to neutralize the objective fairness that the jury is supposed to provide.

Courts have long recognized that other people can be consciously or unconsciously influenced by biases. Potential jurors are asked a series of questions designed to root out possible favoritism in a process known as "voir dire." For example, potential jurors for a landlord-tenant trial might be asked if they have ever been evicted.

When a possible bias is discovered during this questioning, the judge and lawyers usually ask the potential juror whether he or she can overcome it and render a verdict based only on the evidence presented. If the answer is no, or the bias appears to be so deep that no reasonable person could over-

come it, the judge will dismiss the juror outright. If the answer is yes, the judge and attorneys may let the juror remain on the jury, depending on their assessment of the juror's sincerity.

This process ensures that people most likely to be biased will not serve as jurors in a case, and alerts the jurors already chosen to guard against letting their bias affect their decision.

A similar process is badly needed to expose a judge's biases. Today, judges routinely hear cases in which they are at serious risk of being influenced by their personal prejudices, friendships, political debts and campaign contributions. Judicial bias may run from the creepingly subtle to the damningly blatant:

- A judge hearing a child support dispute may have just finished locking horns with an ex-spouse in a bitter battle over child support.
- A judge who is a landlord with a cynical attitude toward tenants may cheerfully preside over an eviction lawsuit.

■ A judge who has received a campaign contribution from a lawyer may rule favorably on that attorney's cases or be tough on lawyers who supported an opponent.

But under the current ethics system, judges are required to inform the parties and perhaps disqualify themselves from hearing a case only in three situations: when they independently conclude that they can't be fair, when they have a financial interest in the outcome, or when they are related to one of the parties or their attorneys.

The reason judges are not subjected to the same stringent bias disclosure rules as are jurors is simple: Judges presume that they are wise enough and objective enough to be able to recognize and correct their own biases without oversight or disclosure. An occasional judge may be able to do this, but most, like the rest of us, cannot.

Judges don't ascend the bench because of demonstrated wisdom, insight and fairness. Most are appointed because they knew the right politician, or were elected because of their ability to raise substantial campaign funds.

WHAT TO DO

To help assure that a dispute headed for a trial will receive an unbiased hearing, the judge should fill in and distribute a two-part disclosure statement to all parties named in a case and the attorneys representing them.

Part 1 would require the judge to answer some basic questions in every type of case, such as:

■ Are you related to or acquainted with the parties or the lawyers in the case?

■ Do you have outside knowledge of the facts in the case that would affect your ability to judge it fairly?

■ Do you have any economic interest in the outcome of the case?

■ Do you know of any other reason that might render you unable to be fair in the case?

The second part of the form would contain the same questions that are put to jurors in a jury trial. It would elicit attitudes or information that might result in more elusive judicial bias in the particular type of case being tried. For instance, in a trial for medical malpractice, the judge and attorneys would likely agree that the judge should disclose if he or she:

■ was related to a doctor who had been sued for malpractice;

■ had ever sued a doctor; or

■ knew any victims of malpractice.

In this example, if the judge had sued a doctor for malpractice, the lawyer representing the hospital might reasonably conclude that the judge was biased against hospitals and request a different judge. As usually happens with biased jurors, a judge who decided that he or she could overcome this possible bias could legally remain on the case but at least proceed with some insight. But this decision could be the basis for an appeal if the party who complains about the bias could show that it may have substantially affected the judge's decision or behavior in the court.

This would not impose much of a burden on judges. In jury trials, with increasing frequency, judges voir dire the jury themselves after meeting with the attorneys to formulate the basic questions. This type of meeting could be held in court trials as well, and in both kinds of trials the judge would answer the questions.

The law, in its egalitarianism, forbids the rich as well as the poor to sleep under bridges, to beg in the streets and to steal bread.

—Anatole France

13 Provide Legal Help for the Poor

Our country is founded on the principle of "justice for all" under the law. But it requires people to buy their way into the legal system by hiring lawyers. Many people who cannot afford to pay the price are shut out of the system.

Over the last quarter century, the small, federally-funded Legal Services Program has existed to provide legal help to the poor. But despite the efforts of many committed people, the results have been disappointing. Most low-income people go without help for their day-to-day legal needs. They can't afford basic services, such as a divorce, guardianship, adoption or eviction defense. Some people argue that the current $300 million program simply needs more money to be successful, but this is naive. It would take billions to do the job—a sum that neither the federal nor state governments are likely to authorize anytime between now and the year 3000.

And lawyers who do volunteer legal work do not adequately deliver the services low-income people so desperately need. Those who contribute free services make a difference in a handful of cases, but when their charity is spread over the millions who need assistance, it's about as effective as dealing with the problem of hunger by having the affluent dole out their table scraps. More important, the poor shouldn't have to depend on charity for access to the legal system.

WHAT TO DO

There is a workable way to provide legal services to the poor: Set up neighborhood law clinics staffed by trained, competent non-lawyers. They could provide a wide range of legal services that are now unavailable to most low-income people, including help with probate, traffic tickets, wills and other problems.

Lawyers, of course, are horrified by this proposal. Typically, they protest that having a non-lawyer do legal work is akin to hiring a mechanic to do brain surgery. But most legal tasks undertaken in existing legal services offices are handled, start to finish, by legal secretaries and paralegals. Indeed, even in prestigious private law firms, high-priced lawyers do next to none of the paperwork. This makes good sense, because filing papers to get an uncontested divorce or bankruptcy, opposing an eviction or appealing a denial of unemployment benefits routinely consists primarily of repetitive paperwork.

Some critics of non-lawyer legal service providers argue that it's important to at least provide supervision by a highly-trained lawyer. This completely ignores the fact that few lawyers have the necessary skills. Lawyers do not learn to provide good quality basic legal services in law school, nor are they tested for this skill in bar exams. In fact, new legal services lawyers learn how to deal with poverty law issues from the secretaries and paralegals who have done it for years, not the other way around.

Many still maintain that even if paralegals can handle some simple tasks, allowing them to provide services to low-income people institutionalizes a dual standard: The middle class can choose lawyers, while the poor must scrape by with paralegals. This is just plain wrong.

First, there is no reason to think that trained non-lawyers provide inferior services. Even the American Bar Association has conceded that the middle class, increasingly unable to buy legal help from lawyers, is turning to independent paralegals to provide cost-effective help with routine legal services such as divorces, bankruptcies, child support modifications and wills.

So, if the middle class can gain access to law by replacing lawyers with paralegals, why can't the poor?

The principal reason is that it's currently illegal for non-lawyers to provide legal advice because practicing law without a license is a crime. Independent paralegals avoid prosecution by claiming that they type legal forms under the direction of their customers. No such argument will work for a full-service, low-income legal clinic; the unauthorized practice laws must be abolished.

Staffing legal clinics with paralegals rather than lawyers will reduce costs of legal clinics, but even so, they will cost plenty. With no new significant major government funding in the offing, a bootstrap approach will be necessary to pay for salaries, operations, training and other other costs inherent in running a large program. Here's how to raise the money:

Existing federal funds. A high level of staff training would be required to provide excellent services and to quiet lawyer critics. The $300 million budget of the existing Legal Services Program should be used to pay for classroom instruction, on-the-job materials, continuing education and for monitoring neighborhood offices to be sure they are delivering top-notch services.

User fees. The biggest cost would be for staff salaries and day-to-day operating costs such as rent and office supplies. The bulk of these costs could be covered by charging customers modest fees. Non-lawyer legal typing services in California have demonstrated that many routine actions such as bankruptcy and divorce can be profitably handled for less than $100—an amount within the reach of many low-income people.

Tax lawyer services. Outside money will be required to provide legal help to those whose incomes are so low they can't afford to pay anything. One method of raising needed funds, suggested by Robert Gnaizda of San Francisco's Public Advocates, is to tax legal services provided by big firms, much as other sales are taxed. Money raised could be spread among non-lawyer clinics based on the number of indigent people they serve. No new tax is popular, but because this one could be a substitute for lawyers doing volunteer work, they would likely support it.

The minute you read something you don't understand, you can be almost sure it was drawn up by a lawyer.

—Will Rogers

14 Take Lawyers Out of House Sales

In most states, each time a house is sold, the buyer and seller must pay lawyers to represent them. It's a vicious, billion-dollar protection racket: Lawyer-dominated state legislatures pass laws that result in buyers and sellers having to pay lawyers to do little or nothing.

Hiring lawyers to preside over a house closing is required by law or custom in most east coast and midwestern states. Real estate professionals who help buyers or sellers transfer title without a lawyer could be found guilty of practicing law without a license—usually a criminal offense. And people who try to represent themselves typically find that banks, lenders and title companies insist that they hire a lawyer.

But requiring lawyers to represent a buyer and seller at a routine house sale is as unnecessary as it is expensive. At closings, lawyers' work consists primarily of reviewing and sometimes preparing standard forms, including the purchase contract and escrow instructions. Most of the paperwork consists of fill-in-the-blanks forms. All can ably be handled by real estate brokers and salespeople, at no additional charge.

Real estate professionals already deal with all the issues covered in these documents as part of their normal duties. In California and several other states, where no law prohibits real estate professionals from handling real estate transfers, few people hire lawyers, and there is no evidence that they suffer legal problems as a result.

Nevertheless, lawyers cling tenaciously to the laws that prohibit buyers and sellers from doing without their services. Without legal advice, lawyers claim, people risk being hurt because they don't understand the technical details of the sale contract, escrow rules or title insurance. If they have a point, it's only that legal language and technicalities are needlessly confusing.

The solution is to rewrite the laws and documents so they can be easily understood by everyone, not to require that lawyers decipher them.

If a possibly thorny legal issue is discovered—for example, a zoning problem or an unexpected lien or easement, legal help is always an option for those who want it. But an occasional problem is no excuse to require every house purchaser and seller to pay thousands of dollars to lawyers.

WHAT TO DO

Here are some changes that would go far toward cleaning up the house-closing racket:

- Repeal all state laws and regulations that require lawyers to participate in house transactions or that make it illegal for real estate professionals and other non-lawyers to handle them.
- Require that all paperwork routinely involved in house transfers be written in plain English. Documents should be accompanied by detailed and easy-to-understand materials describing the laws and customs involved in buying or selling a house.
- Require that title insurance policies be written to guarantee that a purchaser's ownership of real property is free and clear. Currently, many policies protect only the lender from defects in title. Protecting the buyer this way would eliminate much of the risk of the transaction and reduce the need for lawyers.

NO LAWYERS REQUIRED IN WASHINGTON

The Supreme Court of Washington has expressly recognized the lawyers' monopoly on real estate transactions for what it is: a consumer fraud. The court ruled in 1985 that buyers and sellers had the right to choose a non-lawyer to handle the paperwork necessary for a property transfer.

In the case, *Cultum v. Heritage House Realtors* (694 P.2d 630), a real estate agent prepared a standard form purchase/sale contract for a customer who wanted to buy a house. The contract, originally drafted by a lawyer, contained boxes and blanks for necessary information. The purchaser changed her mind about the house and sued Heritage House under Washington's Consumer Protection Law, seeking damages based on the agent's "unauthorized practice of law."

The Washington Supreme Court ended the lawyer monopoly over preparing paperwork for real estate closings by ruling that licensed real estate professionals who prepare house sale contracts are not practicing law. The court said:

> For a long time, suppression of the practice of law by nonlawyers has been proclaimed to be in the public interest, a necessary protection against incompetence, divided loyalties and other evils. It is now clear, however, as several other courts have concluded, that there are other important interests involved. These interests include:
>
> 1. The ready availability of legal services.
> 2. Using the full range of services that other professions and businesses can provide.
> 3. Limiting costs.
> 4. Public convenience.
> 5. Allowing licensed brokers and salespersons to participate in an activity in which they have special training and experience.
> 6. The interest of brokers and salespersons in drafting form earnest money agreements which are incidental and necessary to the main business of brokers and salespersons.
>
> . . . We no longer believe that the supposed benefits to the public from the lawyers' monopoly on performing legal services justifies limiting the public's freedom of choice. The public has the right to use the full range of services that brokers and salespersons can provide.

*Every seventh year you shall practice
remission of debts. This shall be the
nature of the remission: Every creditor shall
remit the due that he claims from his
neighbor; he shall not dun his neighbor or
kinsman.*

—Deuteronomy 15:1-2

Simplify Bankruptcy

People who get into debt over their heads are offered a second chance by our bankruptcy laws. Unfortunately, the bankruptcy process is more complicated, expensive and legalistic than it needs to be. And too often, the interests of debtors are sacrificed to those of lawyers.

Consumers can file for one of two types of bankruptcy. The Chapter 7 bankruptcy system gives debtors a fresh start by canceling (discharging) most of their debts. In exchange, some of a debtor's property is sold to pay creditors part of what they're owed. Chapter 13 bankruptcy is more complicated. The debtor usually doesn't have to give up any property, but must agree to pay a portion of the debts over several years in exchange for the rest being wiped out.

Both forms of debt relief are handled in federal bankruptcy court. Someone who files for bankruptcy need only fill out several fairly straightforward forms showing assets, debts, income and expenses, and a list of property the debtor claims he or she is legally entitled to keep. Court appearances before a judge are rarely required. Most debtors go to court only once—to answer a few questions posed to them by a creditor or the bankruptcy trustee, the official handling the case for the court.

But because only lawyers are allowed to represent people in a federal court, the debtor must either hire an attorney or handle the case alone. Going it alone is very difficult for people who lack good reading skills or the requisite knowledge and self-confidence. In some communities, they can get help with paperwork and filing from non-lawyer typing services for about $100 a case, but many people live in areas where this option isn't available.

Most people, as a result, hire a lawyer to handle their legal paperwork and appear with them in court. Allowing for the fact that about half of the cases are complex enough to require a lawyer's services, still roughly $180 million is unnecessarily consumed by bankruptcy lawyers each year. That astounding number is computed like this: Of the 600,000 people who file for bankruptcy every year, 300,000 pay their lawyers to handle complex cases. The other 300,000 each pay an attorney about $600 that could be better spent to repay creditors or help debtors start over.

WHAT TO DO

An administrative agency, staffed by bankruptcy experts, should be created to take the place of the bankruptcy court. Lawyers and courts should be eliminated except for relatively rare situations when a dispute constitutionally must be handled in court.

The new agency would:

- create user-friendly instructions to help people complete bankruptcy forms without professional assistance, and provide free guidance for those who needed help;
- check forms for completeness and accuracy before the debtors filed them; and
- solicit any additional information needed from the debtor by telephone or mail.

As with the present system, notice of the bankruptcy filing would be sent to all creditors the debtor listed. The creditors could either use their own computers to examine the papers directly by means of a modem and telephone line, or receive a printout of the papers upon request. The creditors would be given a reasonable time to respond.

A bankruptcy examiner would then issue a proposed order based on the law and the information provided by the debtor and creditors. If the examiner concluded the debtor could repay the debts, the order would invite the debtor to submit a repayment plan. If not, the order would identify the debts to be canceled and the property to be sold.

If the debtor or a creditor disagreed with the examiner's order, or wished to raise some other issue—such as whether a particular debt should be canceled—mediation services from a neutral third person would be available. If this failed, the dispute would be resolved in an informal administrative hearing.

Like the current bankruptcy court system, this new system would be funded by bankruptcy filing fees—which should be substantially reduced due to the new system's increased efficiency in handling routine bankruptcy cases.

BANKRUPTCY: IT CAN HAPPEN TO ANYONE

Who files for bankruptcy, and why? According to a recent comprehensive study of consumer bankruptcy filings, bankrupt people are much like any of us—not exceptionally poor, not particularly reckless in their borrowing habits. The one characteristic they share is a recent, major disruption in income—caused by a job loss, small business failure or injury.

The truth is, lots of us are but a few missed paychecks away from bankruptcy.

For a unique view of the bankruptcy process, see *As We Forgive Our Debtors*, by Theresa A. Sullivan, Elizabeth Warren and Jay Lawrence Westbrook (Oxford University Press 1989).

16 Take Divorce Out of Court

Getting divorced can be a wrenching process, made worse by intrusive, lengthy, expensive and hostile legal proceedings. Lawyers, who profit from the misery of divorcing couples—the more fighting, the more profit—have resisted the fundamental reforms necessary to civilize the process.

Historically, the main problem with divorce proceedings has been their preoccupation with fault. That encourages acrimony and finger-pointing between divorcing spouses, and creates an atmosphere so poisonous that it makes it difficult to cooperate in the future to raise children. Many states have solved this problem with no-fault divorce laws, which allow a couple to divorce without first having to prove that one person was at fault.

Unfortunately, a number of other states allow no-fault divorce only after a long separation, or if there are no children—qualifications most people don't meet. In these states, spouses may have to prove "grounds" for the divorce. That means they must testify in court about some act of "mental cruelty" or other legally-acceptable ground, such as desertion. This charade virtually mandates perjury and makes a mockery of the court process.

Even in states that provide no-fault divorce with no strings attached, getting a divorce, which can involve filing up to a dozen court forms and making one or more court appearances, is needlessly complicated. Most people hire lawyers to help them though it.

Another reason panicked divorcing couples run to lawyers is the complexity of divorce laws—the rules about property division, child support and so on. While this could as well be said about many other areas of the law, it's particularly harmful in divorce because so many couples, already anxious and vulnerable, receive all sorts of frightening misinformation from well-meaning friends and family members.

Driven by the almighty fee, lawyers have an overwhelming economic incentive to give bad advice. Too often they instigate or encourage aggressive legal maneuvers, delays and even perjured testimony, which can make even the most cordial of uncouplings degenerate into a battle.

Yet another negative in the current system—one that also plays into the hands of litigation-happy lawyers—is that judges have too much discretion to set child and spousal support levels, and even, in some states, to divide couples' property. When similar cases are decided differently, according to the whims and preferences of a particular judge, it doesn't take long for the word to get around.

One judge is said to be hard on women while another is reputed to consistently award high child support. This encourages people to shop for the right lawyer, who can manipulate the process so their case comes before the right judge or commissioner.

WHAT TO DO

Divorce laws need to be cleaner, less adversarial and administered in a consistent, evenhanded way. Good information, positive reinforcement for couples who are trying to cooperate and free publicly-funded mediation of disputes should be hallmarks of the new system. In addition, procedures should be easy enough to make hiring a lawyer a truly discretionary decision.

Fault should be eliminated as a prerequisite for divorce in all states, no matter how long the couple has been separated and regardless of whether they have any children.

The current system could be replaced by a simple administrative process of de-registering marriages. To marry, you need only state your name, age and address, get a few simple medical tests and pay a small fee. When both parties are willing, divorce should be even easier; you don't need the tests. Removing divorce from court would free many couples— particularly younger ones in short marriages who have little property and no children—from doing anything more than de-registering.

Even important questions that often accompany divorce, such as how to divide property and determine child custody and support, do not require a complicated court-controlled process. These very personal issues, which are best decided by the people involved, should be separated from the divorce itself and handled administratively. For example, a couple having difficulty valuing property to divide it fairly should be able to meet with a trained public official who can help them.

To make the divorce process more fair and predictable, lawmakers should standardize rules for property division, child support and alimony, publicize them and stick to them doggedly.

In addition to simplifying procedures, courts should ensure that people know and understand basics of divorce law— the rules that govern property division, alimony and child support and custody. They could go a long way toward doing this by distributing free pamphlets that clearly explain the law.

A GOOD BOOK IS WELL WORTH THE PRICE
From a letter to Nolo Press:

My husband and I had been separated for almost four years. We had no minor children and the property settlement had already been worked out in our separation agreement. He wanted the divorce and so did I. There was no alimony or cash settlement. I contacted lawyers in the Washington, DC area, and was quoted prices ranging from $1,200 to $2,400—for an uncontested divorce. I was told that one attorney would have to be retained for my husband and another for me, papers would have to be served on him by a sheriff in Washington state (he was in the Navy and stationed there at the time) and that prices would probably go higher because of the joint-state residence factor. (His home of record is Alabama.)

[In desperation, she bought a self-help book, with forms and directions for how to file an uncontested divorce.]

The commissioner handling the case tacked $30 on to the fee that I had been quoted over the phone one week earlier. She told me that the increase was because I didn't have an attorney and she would have to do extra work.

Even with her inflated charges, the entire divorce came to $220. That included court costs, the commissioner's fee, the court reporter's fee, filing fees and the fees for certified mail to my husband. Oh—the cost of the book was additional.

Knowledge and human power are synonymous.

—Francis Bacon

17 Computerize the Law

Computers are powerful tools that could bring legal information and forms to the public easily and efficiently, but their promise has largely been ignored. Only lawyers have the expertise—and the money—to use most existing legal computer programs.

Accomplishing a wide array of legal tasks—bankruptcy, incorporation, name change, divorce or probate, for example—requires only understanding routine court procedures and preparing the right paperwork. The average person, given access to the right materials and instructions on how to fill them out, is perfectly capable of handling the job.

Unfortunately, getting the necessary information and instructions can be nearly impossible. Courts occasionally furnish standardized forms, but almost never provide instructions. Form books written for lawyers can be hard to find outside of a lawyer's office or law library—and even harder to use. Self-help law books may not cover the particular subject or may be too limited in an individual situation.

One way that these significant barriers to legal access could quickly be eliminated is by making the computer the great equalizer, the ultimate self-help law filing cabinet. Computer access to legal forms and information isn't as far-fetched as it may sound. Computers can already accommodate enough information to fill a law library, thanks to mass-information storage and retrieval technologies such as laser-driven compact disks and computer hard disks. Programming techniques are already available to make the information and forms readily accessible to the public in a variety of formats.

One group of lawyers that runs a telephone legal advice service—Telelawyer—relies on a menu-driven legal information database that quickly produces narrowly focused answers to a wide variety of legal questions. Self-help law programs designed to use with personal computers already help people make wills, incorporate their businesses and write contracts. Lawyers regularly use software programs and specialized databases to do research and prepare documents.

WHAT TO DO

A computerized legal information and forms system should be available to the general public in courthouses and public libraries.

A cornerstone of such a system would be consumer-oriented computer databases. User-friendly computer programs would connect the database to answer questions on a variety of common legal subjects. Someone who wanted guidance in completing a legal task would be guided by the computer, step-by-step, through the task. The computer would produce all necessary forms and provide instructions for filling them in and filing them.

Consumers who just needed information could first choose a general topic. Then they would gradually narrow their search, proceeding through a series of menus, until they found the answers they needed. For instance, suppose Paul is getting a divorce and wants to find out whether he has to share his government pension with his spouse.

Current computer technology would allow him simply to sift through a menu listing general subject areas. After selecting divorce, he would then be presented with a list of related topics. He would select pensions from this list and encounter a third menu with types of pensions. He would select the entry for his pension and receive a clear statement of the rule used by his state's divorce court for that type of pension.

If Paul wanted assistance with divorce paperwork, he would call up the procedure part of the divorce database and be presented with the necessary forms, to be filled in on the screen. When necessary, he could use the help feature of the program to get line-by-line instructions. When finished, Paul could print out the forms, ready to be filed with the court. The computer would also print out instructions for signing, serving and filing them.

Another approach would permit Paul to type in a plain-English question, such as: "Must I share my government pension with my wife if we divorce?" The computer would analyze this question—called parsing—and determine that Paul wants information about pensions and divorce. The computer might then ask Paul to describe his pension, what state he lives in, how long he's been married, and possibly other questions. These answers would also be analyzed.

Implementing a self-help legal computer system will be harder than describing it. Expect little help from lawyers, who currently monopolize legal information and have seen to it that publicly available forms and instructions are rare, even for the simplest task.

But self-help law systems could be profitable to the business that developed them. They could be sold to courts and libraries, which in turn could charge reasonable user fees.

A comprehensive system such as the one described here doesn't exist yet largely because of a lack of imagination. Business people, like so many others, think of law as something that belongs to lawyers. This will change. As legal software programs, such as those already on the market that allow people to form a corporation or write a personnel plan, proliferate and succeed, business will see the opportunity to profit. Along the way, computers could revolutionize public access to the legal system.

The thing to fear is not the law, but the judge.

—Russian proverb

18 Eliminate Bias in the Courts

Our courts are dedicated to the ideal of fairness and equal treatment for all who enter. But many judges bring to the courtroom the same prejudices that taint the society outside their walls—and refuse to acknowledge or remedy the problems it creates.

There is little doubt that bias against women, racial minorities and unpopular minority groups pervades the court system. Corrosive as prejudice is in society at large, it is intolerable in the courts, where all citizens seek justice. A few examples:

■ Studies have found that the severity of a prison sentence is correlated with the race of the criminal's victim. Someone convicted of killing a white person, for example, usually gets a stiffer sentence than someone who kills a person of another race.

■ One Texas judge justified giving a light sentence to a convicted killer because the victim had been gay. Many commentators criticized the judge's candor, but not his prejudice.

■ In some courts, people who use wheelchairs are automatically disqualified from jury duty. They must make special requests if they want to serve. Los Angeles County had to be sued before it would allow hearing-impaired people to serve as jurors.

■ Judges often treat minority and women witnesses, court employees and lawyers without respect. For example, one California judge ordered an attorney—the only woman among a group of seven—to type up a settlement agreement. "Come on sweetheart," urged the judge. "I know you can type."

■ African-American and Hispanic lawyers are often harassed by court officers who assume they are criminal defendants. Judges often call them by their first names and refer to their minority clients as "boy" or "girl."

Such anecdotal evidence is well supported by systematic research. Recent studies, for example, found pervasive gender discrimination in New York, Massachusetts, New Jersey, Rhode Island, Maryland, Nevada and California courts. The result is "more than hurt feelings," the Massachusetts study concluded. These attitudes "affect women's ability to function in the system, and they are linked to unjust outcomes."

Such prejudice also destroys faith in the fairness of the court system. A 1989 New York investigation into racial bias found that many minorities mistrust the state's court system, which is overwhelmingly dominated by whites. In New York City Housing Court, for example, 81% of the tenants are black, but 79% of the judges are white. One woman asked the New York panel to imagine how a black mother feels when she goes into Family Court and sees white clerks, white guards, white psychologists, white correctional officers, white lawyers and white judges.

But despite the mounting evidence, most courts refuse even to acknowledge the problem. This hypocrisy and indifference, on top of the actual unfairness, make a travesty of the legal system's claims to provide equal justice under the law.

WHAT TO DO

To eliminate bias in the courts is, of course, a huge task—probably an impossible one, because courts are run by imperfect humans. And the legal establishment has always been conservative, revering tradition and loathing change. But there is an obvious place to start: judges. Judges, most of whom are white males, control the courts. They set the tone for how employees and people who appear in court are treated. And most important, judges are government employees who can be made accountable to the public.

First, more minority members and women should be appointed to the bench. Judges and other court employees should be trained to recognize and deal with invidious discrimination. Just as judges attend seminars to keep up on the law, they should regularly participate in programs to educate and re-mind them about how to protect the civil rights of the people in their courts. Members of the minorities who face discrimination should be actively involved in designing the curriculum and teaching the programs.

A California commission investigating the problem of gender bias has recommended that judges be given a "fairness manual," covering appropriate behavior toward jurors, employees and other people who appear in court.

That's a good place to start. Among other things, judges should be required to stop lawyers from badgering witnesses or other lawyers, and reprimand or discipline lawyers who make racist, sexist or other discriminatory comments.

To put some teeth into these requirements, the codes of conduct that govern judges should be updated to reflect these concerns. Strict, concrete rules should require scrupulous fairness from judges, and judges who violate the rules should be disciplined. In serious cases, judges should be removed from office.

It's also essential to get more minorities into other, non-judicial positions in the justice system. The people who work as clerks, bailiffs, counselors and other court workers have the most direct contact with the public and have a significant effect on how minorities and women are treated.

19 Write Laws in Plain English

Reading most statutes is like wading through a swamp. At every step, muddy language pulls at you, and thorny cross-references threaten to tear you from your path. Many people are shut out of the legal system because they can't understand the language in which the law is written.

Most laws are written by lawyers. Law is complex, they claim, and laws must be written in mysterious jargon to convey its meaning precisely. But anyone who's ever tried to make sense of a statute knows that such legalese fosters confusion instead of reducing it.

Sometimes legal terms are useful shorthand—but we're not talking about nuclear engineering manuals here. These are the laws that regulate our lives. Obscure terms are rarely necessary, and could always be explained in plain English somewhere in the statute.

The problem with the way most statutes are written is not only that they are full of unfamiliar terms; it's also that they are written poorly.

Here's an example of a Maryland law:

"The Board may appoint, discharge at pleasure, and fix the compensation of the secretary and such clerical force as from time to time in its judgment may be necessary in the administration of this subtitle if it has funds available for the payment of such persons."

The same law, as rewritten into plain English by a group that's tackling the whole set of Maryland statutes: "The Board may em-ploy a staff in accordance with the state budget."

Laws written so that ordinary people can't understand them don't square with what we all learn, from grade school on: that we are responsible for knowing the law. And we *are* responsible, even if the law is incomprehensible. Just try telling a court clerk that you missed a crucial filing deadline because your state's law is written so poorly.

There are three main reasons why most laws read like hieroglyphics.

The first reason is rooted in a belief shared, perhaps unconsciously, by lawyers and legislators: that it doesn't matter that non-lawyers can't read the laws. Many of those who write laws simply assume that someone who wants to know what the law means will ask a lawyer. The legal profession gains much of its status—and profit—from its exclusive access to legal knowledge.

Second, bad writing begets bad writing. Law students learn legal writing by reading the jargon-filled decisions of judges. Imitating that sorry style, they are soon turning out prose packed with "said," "heretofore" and as much Latin as they can come up with.

Third, lobbyists and legislators who have lost a legislative fight over a law may actually want it to be ambiguous. If the wording in a statute is unclear, they may get another chance to argue over its meaning in a later lawsuit.

It should go without saying that people shouldn't have to rely on lawyers, paying through the nose or depending on uncertain charity (free legal services are only sporadically available and only to the very poor), to find out about the law that governs their lives. In a democracy, the laws belong to all. They are written by the legislators we elected. They should be written in the language we speak.

Legal commentators have wrung their hands for years over the poor quality of lawyers' writing, and law professors have proposed new scientific, computer-aided systems for drafting coherent statutes, but states have taken few steps toward making the laws comprehensible.

The plain English statutes passed by a few state legislatures don't apply to the statutes they write themselves. Instead, they require certain kinds of consumer contracts to be written in clear, understandable language. Although commendable, these laws are so limited—many exclude mortgages, deeds and insurance policies—that their practical effect is relatively insignificant.

And more than 20 years ago, President Carter directed federal agencies to make their regulations "as simple and clear as possible." The agencies hired consultants to help, but if federal regulations have become models of clarity, it has escaped most readers' notice.

WHAT TO DO

The solution is so simple that only politicians could miss it: Write our federal, state and local laws and regulations in plain English, so the average person can understand them. Some states have already taken small steps in this direction. California, for example, recently rewrote its small claims court laws to make them understandable to the average person. The task was supervised by the state Department of Consumer Affairs.

All laws, before lawmakers vote on them, should be scrutinized to make sure they are clear, unambiguous and written in everyday language. This wouldn't require adding a costly layer of bureaucracy to the legislative process. Most state legislatures already have a central office for bill-drafting. It shouldn't cost much to shift its priorities toward clarity and cogency.

To guide the people charged with overseeing bill-drafting, a national, nonpartisan citizens' committee should be created. Its job would be to write, publish and distribute common-sense guidelines for legislation. It should establish rules for sentence and paragraph length (statutes are notorious for going on and on and on), vocabulary (you shouldn't need a legal dictionary), grammar and syntax. It could also publish model laws, not for substance but as examples of clear expression.

Finally, there should also be a way for citizens to complain about garbled laws that slip through the system. Complaints could be referred to the bill-drafting committee, which would re-evaluate the clarity of the legislation.

*Did you ever expect a corporation
to have a conscience, when it has no
soul to be damned, and no body to be
kicked?*

—Lord Thurlow
Chancellor of England

Punish Corporate Criminals

Some of society's most destructive criminals—corporations that trash the environment, bilk millions from investors or poison employees—get away with their crimes. If they are caught, they pay small fines and keep going. The people responsible hide behind the corporation and are rarely punished.

The criminal justice system is set up to deal with flesh-and-blood wrongdoers who ply their trade the old-fashioned way: with guns, knives or everyday scams.

But it is almost totally ineffective when it comes to dealing with some of the country's most dangerous criminals: corporations. They may flout environmental regulations, risking the health of unsuspecting citizens. They may expose employees to dangerous working conditions. The victims of these crimes often number in the millions.

Prosecutors who want to punish the crime have a choice: They can go after the culpable decision-makers within the company, or they can put the corporation itself on trial.

For several reasons, they almost always pursue the corporation. Executives of huge multinational corporations are often politically powerful and well-connected. And as a practical matter, in large companies, it's notoriously difficult to pin guilt on specific people. Occasionally, an employee caught red-handed—dumping toxic chemicals down the storm sewer behind a film developing lab, for example—is convicted and sent to jail, but most employees know that they face virtually no risk of jail if they commit crimes in the name of the company.

And many financially pressed prosecutors' offices get a large chunk of their funding from the fines their prosecutions generate. Going after jail sentences instead of big fines would undercut their own budgets.

So instead of going after individuals, prosecutors' strategy has been to charge the corporations and sting them with fines. There are serious problems with this approach. Prosecutions are infrequent—only one in a hundred criminal defendants in federal court is a corporation—and notoriously ineffective at preventing further lawbreaking by the company.

Most fines imposed are so small that they are merely written off as a cost of doing business. Regulatory bodies such as the federal Environmental Protection Agency often threaten big fines for polluters, but then bargain with the companies and reduce the fines—sometimes as much as 97%.

In 1988, fines of $25,000 to $50,000 were common for actions that caused millions of dollars in property or environmental damage or threatened lives and public safety, according to the U.S. Sentencing Commission. Sixty percent of all corporate fines were under $10,000.

Even seemingly large fines may not seriously affect the huge companies responsible for serious crimes such as large-scale environmental contamination or distribution of dangerous products. Unless a big fine exceeds profits from illegal activity or the cost of complying with the law, corporations have little to lose by breaking the law. In 1988, according to the Sentencing Commission, the median fine was only 20% of the loss caused by a corporation's wrongdoing. So even if the corporations are caught and forced to pay a fine, their crime still pays.

For example, if Exxon were fined $1 billion for the recklessness that caused the catastrophic oil spill in Prince William Sound, Alaska in 1989, the giant company might hardly notice it. Exxon's sales for just the first nine months of 1989 were $68 billion.

Those actually punished by fines are shareholders, customers and employees, who ultimately foot the bill. Large fines don't deter the middle and upper managers who make many of the decisions that cause a company to break the law.

The futility of fines as a deterrent is almost universally acknowledged, but big business lobbies hard to keep more effective measures from being implemented. The Sentencing Commission, studying criminal sentences in 1990, was seriously considering recommending stiffer fines and probation for companies convicted of serious crimes. The U.S. Justice Department, which first supported these tougher measures, abruptly changed sides after intensive lobbying from big corporations, including defense contractors and oil companies. The commission put off making a decision.

WHAT TO DO

Two traditional criminal punishments—jail and probation—should be applied to punish corporate criminals.

Jail time for corporate executives would effectively deter corporate crime. To potential white-collar criminals, the threat of doing time carries a visceral punch that fines, even large ones, will never have. As Los Angeles environmental crimes prosecutor David Guthman put it, "Paying big fines doesn't have the impact on businessmen that a day in jail has."

Many of these criminals deserve much more than a day in jail. Their punishment should at least be on a par with the sentences meted out to perpetrators of similarly serious crimes. Perpetuating the current double standard breeds cynicism and mistrust of the criminal justice system.

Probation can be applied to a corporation itself. After a company is convicted of a crime, the judge can set a probation period and appoint probation officers to oversee the company's operations. The court could also order an audit, or order the company to submit a report spelling out its plans to avoid recurrences. That would force a dishonest or dangerous company to change its ways, and possibly its entire structure and decision-making process, and prevent it from engaging in more socially destructive behavior.

The language of the law must not be foreign to the ears of those who are to obey it.

—Judge Learned Hand

21 Make Competent Interpreters Available

People who can't speak English and find themselves in court are often at the mercy of unqualified interpreters. If they cannot understand or participate in what is going on, a fair proceeding is impossible.

Having a skilled interpreter is critical to a fair proceeding. By controlling much of what the defendant, jury, judge and lawyers hear, the interpreter becomes the most powerful person in the courtroom—the only link between a non-English-speaking witness or party and everyone else in the courtroom. A bad job of interpreting can mean that a person loses custody of a child or valuable property, is deported or goes to jail.

Many people who go to court but cannot speak English do not get an interpreter at all. Only criminal defendants are legally entitled to interpreters. Courts are not required to provide interpreters in civil lawsuits such as divorces, for example; non-English speakers must bring along with them to court a relative or friend who can help out.

When an interpreter is used, courts do little to ensure that he or she is competent. The pay is not high enough, in many places, to attract skilled people. Only a few states and the federal courts require court interpreters to have passed a skills test; most courts do not require any evidence of interpreting skill. At most, courts require basic knowledge of languages.

But language experts protest that interpreting is a skill all its own, and being bilingual is no guarantee of interpreting ability. Interpreting, according to a professor who heads the country's first college program for legal interpreters, involves the tricky feat of "communicating across culture." Interpreters must not only faithfully translate word-for-word, but are also required to come up with accurate translations of idiomatic expressions. Court interpreters have the additional burden of translating something often dubbed a language all its own: legal terms.

Many untrained interpreters commit the cardinal sin of summarizing testimony, editing out offensive words or adding their own twists, and skipping over difficult words instead of translating verbatim. The frequent result is a significant change in the meaning or implication of what is said. Of course, someone who doesn't speak English does not know whether the interpreter is doing a good job. Few of the many mistakes are caught. Even then, there is usually no recourse against a judgment that is already final.

Because qualified courtroom interpreters are in short supply, courts often find interpreters on a hit-or-miss basis. Sometimes they rely on bilingual court personnel. Sometimes they are more creative. A California court clerk, for example, once called Chinese restaurants until she found someone to interpret. "He was awfully hard to understand," she later told a reporter.

Predictably, the odds of getting an incompetent interpreter are high. A 1985 New Jersey task force found that only 17% of the interpreters used in that state's courts met its minimum standards. There were significant errors in more than half of all interpreted cases there. Shoddy or nonexistent standards are at least partly to blame: Half of the 500 court interpreters surveyed recently by a San Jose, California newspaper said they had no more than a week's training for their jobs.

But once an interpreter is working in a courtroom, it's rare that anyone present has the skills to evaluate ability or catch mistakes. Among the examples of botched interpreting jobs uncovered by the newspaper's investigation was the case of a Vietnamese immigrant convicted of robbery on the basis of questionable eyewitness identifications. No other evidence linked him to the crime. At trial, his lawyer asked one of the witnesses, who spoke only Hmong, if the robber had facial hair. The jury heard the witness's answer as, "The hair the same." But the interpreter had actually translated the question as: "Was his hair long?" The witness had answered, in Hmong, "Same length as mine." Even after evidence

of the botched translation, the court turned down a request for a new trial.

Even more troubling is the news that some interpreters are downright fraudulent. For example, a San Francisco judge who speaks three Chinese dialects recently said she had several times heard Mandarin-speaking interpreters pretending to interpret Cantonese.

WHAT TO DO

Courts should make competent interpreters available for all proceedings, civil and criminal. And the interpreters should be paid salaries that reflect the skills required and importance of the service they provide.

Courts should employ only interpreters who present objective evidence of competency, such as a proof of passing a rigorous exam. Exams should be tough enough to ensure the competency of those who pass. The exams should emphasize practical interpreting skills, not just rudimentary language abilities.

To ensure a supply of competent interpreters, states should set up certification programs. They should set standards for training programs, which could then be offered by public and private schools. Training should both teach translating skills and instill in students the ethics of the job—for example, that summarizing a speaker's testimony is a serious violation of an interpreter's responsibilities.

Finally, the state agency in charge of testing and certifying interpreters should regularly monitor the courtroom performance of certified interpreters.

22 Help Non-Lawyers Use Law Libraries

Many law libraries are off-limits to non-lawyers, and all are needlessly hard for non-lawyers to use. Without access to a good, usable law library, the public cannot have access to law.

The average person needs dozens of legal questions answered in a lifetime. We may dispute tree ownership with a neighbor, child custody with a former spouse, or last year's taxes with the IRS. Or we may just need to know how to write a valid will, file for divorce or incorporate a small business. The best place to find specific answers is usually the law library.

Unfortunately, it is often impossible for non-lawyers to use this essential information source. For just as law libraries own the law, lawyers own the law libraries. In some places, this is literally true: Lawyers rent the building, buy the books, and for the most part keep the public out. Even law libraries that are publicly funded—in courthouses or public law schools—are run primarily as a resource for law students, lawyers and judges.

Many law libraries, reflecting the elitist attitudes of their lawyer patrons, offer the public no assistance in how to approach the forbidding-looking books. They simply assume that anyone who wants to use the law library already possesses the research skills to track down and make sense of a large body of legal information. But because this arcane skill is taught only in law schools, everyone else is denied access to legal information.

The double standard is often manifested in how library privileges are allotted. Word processing rooms, conference areas and telephones—all extremely helpful in researching and preparing documents—are available to lawyers in many places, but off-limits to self-helpers. Similarly, many law libraries allow lawyers to check out books freely, but demand a deposit from non-lawyers before trusting them with materials.

The bias toward lawyers also shows up in the materials in the library's collection. Almost always, libraries are full of form books and practice manuals written for lawyers, but noticeably lacking in good self-help books and software.

WHAT TO DO

A number of simple reforms would help give citizens meaningful access to law libraries.

First, because public librarians are often asked legal questions, they should be educated about the materials available at law libraries and how non-lawyers can use them.

All law libraries that receive public funds or subsidies, including those run by private colleges, should be open to the public. At law school libraries, students in Advanced Legal Research classes could get course credit for helping self-helpers use the library. Students would have to help someone with a specific legal research project. Students would get practical experience, and the self-helpers would get free assistance.

Every county—or every two or three counties in sparsely-populated areas—should have at least one public law library. These libraries should be open a reasonable number of evening and weekend hours. In larger law libraries, the reference staff should include at least one specialist to assist non-lawyers.

Public law libraries, many of which are chronically strapped for cash, should be funded from consistent, predictable sources. Typically, a percentage of lawsuit filing fees collected is allocated to the local courthouse library. But since lawyers benefit most from law libraries, they should provide a significant amount of the funding. A portion of their annual state bar association dues could be earmarked for public law libraries.

Law libraries should also be redesigned so that the public can more easily use them. Librarians should:

■ Create pamphlets, displays, videos and other material to explain how legal materials are organized and catalogued.

■ Prepare "fast track" outlines of how to do legal research on common problems, such as getting a divorce, increasing child support or coping with a landlord who won't make necessary repairs.

■ Offer short courses on how to use the library, including tours and hands-on exercises.

USING THE LAW LIBRARY

Here are some good tools to help you use the law libary. Most are in large law libraries.

Legal Research: How To Find and Understand the Law, Stephen Elias (Nolo Press). A nontechnical but detailed book, written for non-lawyers. It's especially good on helping you frame research questions and get around the jargon trap.

Legal Research and Writing: Some Starting Points, William P. Statsky (West Publishing). This easy-to-use book contains photographs of law books and simple descriptions of how to use them.

How To Find the Law (9th Ed.), Cohen, Berring and Olson (West Publishing) and *Fundamentals of Legal Research,* Jacobstein and Mersky (Foundation Press). These texts are written for law students and may overwhelm you with detail. Each has a paperback abridgement that contains selected chapters.

The Process of Legal Research: Successful Strategies, Christina L. Kunz (Little Brown). An interesting feature of this book is that librarians discuss how to solve model problems.

Legal Research Made Easy, Robert Berring (Nolo Press/Legal Star). This 2 1/2 hour videotape, designed for non-lawyers, shows you step-by-step how to formulate your legal research question and use the library to find the answer.

If you want to find the law, go to law school.
If you want to find justice, go to small
claims court.

—Paul Rosenthal
Former Legal Aid lawyer

23 Expand Small Claims Court Limits

America's trial court system is costly, constipated and complicated beyond reason. Small claims court, with its simple rules, low cost and easy access for non-lawyers, is potentially a powerful alternative. But unrealistically low dollar limits and restrictions on the types of cases allowed in small claims hobble its usefulness.

The great majority of disputes are easy to understand and require relatively small dollar amounts to resolve. These include spats over auto and home repairs, landlord-tenant issues, unpaid bills and substandard services. It's not worth the time or money to take these disputes to regular court. With attorney fees routinely running upwards of $150 per hour, a dispute must be worth $20,000 before it becomes cost-effective to hire a lawyer. Less, and the transactional costs—including lawyers' and court fees—loom larger than the problem.

And bringing in lawyers doesn't always serve the cause of justice. According to California Superior Court Judge Roderic Duncan:

"People are much more likely to stand up and tell the unvarnished version of what happened when they represent themselves. Something about a lawyer being in the process, coaching people to alter their stories, results in victory becoming more important than telling the truth."

Routine disputes are best settled by the people involved, outside of the traditional court system. Mediation—discussions with a neutral third person who tries to help those in dispute reach an agreement—is one possibility. But if people can't agree, they often turn to small claims court. Unfortunately, because of ridiculously low dollar limits ($2,500 or less in most states), people with claims worth between $2,500 and $20,000 face a miserable choice. They can kiss off a good chunk of their potential recovery by reducing their claim to the small claims court maximum, try to represent themselves in a regular lawyer-controlled trial court, or hire a lawyer even though the fees charged are likely to be more than what they win.

Assume, for example, that a homeowner and a contractor disagree about whether a $20,000 kitchen remodeling job was done properly. Angry words are exchanged, and attempts to compromise prove futile. Each person hires a lawyer and the case goes to trial two years later. The lawyers each bill for 40 hours of time at $150 per hour—costing each side $6,000. Court fees, document preparation and expert witness fees add another $1,000 each. Assume now that the homeowner wins a partial victory—he need only pay the contractor $14,000 for the substandard work. Add that to the $7,000 in legal expenses, and the homeowner is out-of-pocket $21,000. The contractor fares no better, netting only $7,000 out of the $20,000, once legal fees are paid. Both sides lose—and spend needless hours and energy fighting in the process.

If the same case were defended in small claims court, both the homeowner and contractor would have a much better shot at justice. Filing fees would amount to about $25, and each side could choose whether to spend a few hundred dollars to have the kitchen work evaluated by an expert witness. The case would then be heard within six weeks of filing, with each side getting the chance to have its say and present evidence. By keeping costs low, both parties benefit almost no matter what the small claims judge decides. For example, even if the judge only knocked 10% off the contractor's bill, as opposed to 30% in the scenario above, the homeowner would pay a total of $18,000 plus a few dollars in fees as opposed to $21,000.

WHAT TO DO

The small claims court dollar limit should be raised to $20,000 in every state—an amount high enough to allow most consumer and small business disputes to be resolved in court without lawyers.

Also, most small claims courts allow only claims for money, barring all sorts of cases that cry out for resolution. The power of small claims court judges should be expanded so that they can order a neighbor to remove a dangerous tree or tell a tenant who fails to pay the rent to vacate an apartment.

Lawyers should be banned from small claims court, except when appearing for themselves.

And finally, consumers should be better educated about how to use small claims court through self-help pamphlets, audios and videos available from the court clerk. An in-person advisor program, like the one currently in place in California, could greatly aid those using the courts. These programs could be funded at no taxpayer cost by slightly increasing the fee to file a small claims case.

THE CALIFORNIA SMALL CLAIMS ADVISOR PROGRAM

When a small claims court case is filed in California, a few dollars of the filing fee goes to the small claims advisor program. In more populous counties, a trained consumer advocate provides free counseling to any person involved in a small claims suit. In rural counties, phone-in counseling is provided.

Small claims court advisors, who are particularly helpful to first-time filers, routinely counsel both plaintiffs and defendants on how to research the law, prepare evidence and appear in court. The success of this program in helping inexperienced litigants was an important factor in the California legislature's recent decision to raise the small claims dollar limit to $5,000.

"Many people who bring small claims suits don't have a clue as to how to collect when they win," according to Jeanne Stott, the small claims legal advisor in San Francisco. "A few minutes of counseling can often remedy this and help people see that small claims court can really produce a tangible result."

Suits at court are like winter nights, long and wearisome.

—Thomas Deloney
English ballad writer

24 Speed Up Civil Lawsuits

File a civil lawsuit today, and it may take a year—or five years—to get to trial. Not only does such delay cause needless inconvenience and anxiety, it severely impairs our courts' ability to do justice.

The U.S. Constitution guarantees criminal defendants a speedy trial. But there is no such guarantee for people involved in civil cases, which typically drag on for years. A dispute over who is at fault in a car accident might take three to five years before it's resolved in court.

The most ingrained reason civil suits take so long is that courts and growing judicial bureaucracies are administered by judges. Judges are lawyers who were appointed or elected to their positions for reasons other than administrative skills and training.

Unfortunately, the argument that judges should stick to judging and hire someone else to speed things up gains little credence because most judges assert their constitutional right to run their courtrooms their own way. Most are ill-equipped.

Urban courts are big businesses, many with up to 50 courtrooms operating simultaneously. On a typical day, everything from divorces to securities fraud cases must be heard. Just getting the right people to the right room is a daunting job. Making the whole system run efficiently is far more difficult. By comparison, in a large medical system where administration has been taken away from doctors and turned over to trained public administrators, a doctor is expected to see a certain number of patients in a day.

But, judges, who typically control their own schedules, proceed at self-dictated paces—and handle far less work than they could.

Unfortunately, the problem of poor judicial administration isn't limited to how and when judges work. In many courthouses, the most contested and time-consuming meetings involve who will get the plum assignments, how much is budgeted for new furniture and who gets the August vacations.

And when lawyers are paid by the hour, their motive for pokiness is as obvious as it is insidious. When lawyers work on a contingency fee basis—meaning that they get paid only if and when their client wins—you'd think they would move faster. After all, the sooner the case concludes, the sooner they get paid. But even here, lawyers are often frustratingly slow. This time the reason is psychological—many lawyers hate the hard work and stress of trials. Better to fill a few years with routine and often worthless motions and depositions. When a case gets old enough, similarly-motivated lawyers on the other side are likely to agree to settle out of court.

Judges help this game along, often routinely granting lawyers' requests for extensions of time.

A final reason why courts can't cope with their caseloads connects directly to the political mood of getting tough on crime. Legislators have created ever more ways for people to go to jail. The "war on drugs" has swamped the judicial system, much as it's overwhelmed police and prisons. For example, drug cases in federal court jumped 270% from 1980 to 1989. In some areas, judges now spend up to 80% of their time handling the criminal side of their dockets. That in turn has meant that civil cases, which get lower priority, are pushed aside.

WHAT TO DO

To provide every citizen with a meaningful day in court, courts must hire skilled administrators and give them authority to make fundamental changes. Courts could handle a larger volume of work far faster. For example, in arbitration and private court settings, eliminating complicated rules of evidence, streamlining procedures, placing tight checks on lawyer posturing and paying judges only for the work they do means that disputes are considered far faster than in court. Political leverage could force reluctant judges to act. Legislatures could withhold funds necessary to fund more courts and judges until structural reforms are instituted.

Speeding up lawyers requires a three-pronged approach. The first is to simplify and shorten the pre-trial "discovery" process in which each side seeks information about the other's case. There is no reason lawyers can't do this in months rather than years.

Second, and perhaps more important, courts should do more to enforce strict deadlines on each step of the process. Requests for extensions should be denied unless there are truly extenuating circumstances. Lawyers who don't meet the deadlines and who delay litigation with frivolous arguments or procedures should be subject to discipline, which in serious and repeated instances could mean losing their law licenses.

Third, lawyers should be required to give each client an up-front estimate of how long a lawsuit will take, including estimates of the time necessary to complete each major stage. If a case moves more slowly than this estimate, the client should receive a written explanation and a new time estimate. The computerized case management systems already used by many law offices make this cheap and easy. Forcing lawyers to do it would give them an incentive to expedite cases rather than explain delays to clients.

Finally, how do courts dig themselves out from under the avalanche of drug and other high-profile criminal cases? One possibility is to decriminalize certain activities now treated as crimes, such as drug addiction, and deal with them through our health system. Another possibility is to expand the number of courts and judges. And a third approach is to remove other cases, such as uncontested divorces, from the court system to make more room.

Laws do not persuade just because they threaten.

—Seneca

25 Do Away with Punitive Damages

Thousands of businesses have closed or curtailed operations because they fear lawsuits and can't afford liability insurance. More worrisome, the fear of huge punitive damages awards has kept a number of potentially useful new products out of the U.S. marketplace.

A jury in a personal injury case must decide whether the person being sued, the defendant, caused the victim's injury. If so, the next question is how much money is needed to compensate the victim. The defendant is ordered to pay that amount, called damages.

But a wild card can change that result drastically: punitive damages. If a jury finds that the harm was caused maliciously or intentionally, it can punish the defendant, setting an amount of damages above what's necessary to compensate the victim. The jury can award any amount of these punitive damages and is free to take into account the wealth of the defendant. The richer the defendant, the theory goes, the bigger the amount needed to make an impact. Appeals courts sometimes reduce punitive damages awards, but they still tend to be hefty—often, several times the amount of the other damages claimed.

There are several serious problems inherent in allowing punitive damages.

■ For any endeavor where there is a perceived risk of high punitive damages awards, from renting bicycles to running an ice rink, liability insurance becomes prohibitively expensive or impossible to get. So business owners simply stop high-risk activities. If you doubt this, try and remember the last time you saw a diving board at a public swimming pool.

■ Judgments for huge dollar amounts are commonly pinned on defendants arbitrarily, defeating the reason they are supposedly awarded—to punish and deter bad or dangerous conduct.

■ Trial lawyers urge juries to focus on the needs of suffering victims, not on whether the defendant's conduct was truly bad. For example, manufacturers of the Sabin polio vaccine had to pay huge punitive damages awards in the mid-1980s to some people who took the vaccine. This happened even though the U.S. government, after considering the risks, had recommended the vaccine because it provided far better immunity than others.

■ The possibility of large punitive damages often slows down the introduction of new products. The price of innovation is that, inevitably, some mistakes will be made. Victims of these mistakes should be compensated, but honest innovators should not be punished.

Proponents of punitive damages argue that the mere possibility that they may be awarded deters bad conduct in some situations, such as when a manufacturer is tempted to sell a product it hasn't thoroughly tested or knows may be unsafe. But because punitive damages are awarded so arbitrarily, a manufacturer cannot predict when it may be at risk. It is far more likely to be deterred by the fact that it will have to compensate anyone to protect injuries.

The punitive damages system continues to exist because lawyers get rich from it. Lawyers make lots of money in contingency fees—commonly, they get 30% to 50% of the award—by convincing juries to pin huge judgments on defendants rich enough to pay. And trial lawyers' groups spend freely to lobby state legislatures and battle in court to keep the system. If lawyers withdrew their opposition, punitive damages would fail at once.

Recently, in response to critics, some states have capped punitive damages at a certain amount, such as $250,000. Others have applied caps to certain types of cases such as medical malpractice. While caps may help rein in the greed of trial lawyers, they make little sense. After all, if punitive damages don't truly deter bad conduct, but serve primarily as a trial lawyer benefit fund, the legal profession would likely try to make up the difference by filing more lawsuits.

WHAT TO DO

Punitive damages should be eliminated. Where convincing evidence shows that a defendant's conduct was truly bad—fraudulent, or a willful violation of health and safety laws—the trial jury should have the power to recommend that state and local prosecutors press criminal charges or seek civil fines. It is more fair to have fines paid to the public treasury than to a victim, who has already been compensated for actual losses. To further ensure the jury's recommendation is taken seriously, the prosecutor should be required either to follow it or explain in writing why it is not followed.

THE FICKLE FINGER OF BLAME

A recent Alabama case is a good example of punitive damages run amok. In that case, Lemmie Ruffin, an insurance agent, sold group health and life insurance policies to cover several employees of Roosevelt City, Alabama. Their life insurance was placed with Pacific Mutual Life Insurance and the health insurance with Union Fidelity Life Insurance, but Ruffin told the city all the insurance was with Pacific Mutual. After a few months, Ruffin began pocketing the insurance premium money. The life and health policies were canceled, but the companies never notified the employees; they just notified Ruffin.

During this time, Cleopatra Haslip, who was covered by the health plan, became ill and incurred medical bills of $3,100. Because she had no insurance and couldn't pay them, the bill was turned over to a collection agency and her credit suffered.

Haslip and several other people in the failed insurance plan sued Ruffin and Pacific Mutual—which did not even sell health insurance—claiming fraud. A jury awarded Haslip her direct economic loss. And an extra $1 million in punitive damages.

[Haslip v. Pacific Mutual Life Insurance Co., 553 So.2d 537 (Ala. 1989)]

26 Allow People To Die with Dignity

At least 10,000 Americans are suspended, through medical machinations, between life and death in a persistent vegetative state. Yet the law cruelly denies these people a simple way to express their final, simple wish: the right to die with dignity.

Most people now accept the definition of death as the moment the brain stops functioning. But medical technology careens on, leaving the laws and understanding far behind. Patients caught in the fray are those not technically brain-dead, but living in a persistent vegetative state, permanently unconscious with no awareness of themselves or their environments.

Family members and loved ones—torn between the desire to help the terminal patient fight the disease and letting death end the struggle—suffer terribly.

Physicians, too, are caught. Stopping medical care is seen by some as an admission of defeat. And some fear that a patient's family, once past the grieving stage, will sue the doctor for failing to do everything possible to preserve a life.

Then there is the matter of money. Medical costs in this country are exorbitant and getting steeper—$541 billion in 1990, a projected $1.5 trillion in 2000. Almost unbelievably, about 60% of those costs are incurred during the last three months of life. The cost of keeping someone "alive"—betubed, monitored, medically dependent—runs as high as $1,000 a day. It is money that could save many lives if spent on care for AIDS patients or a host of other dollar-starved programs. Few families and loved ones can foot such a bill, and tapped-out government health care funds provide little back-up.

In 1990, the U.S. Supreme Court, in *Cruzan v. Missouri Department of Health,* ruled that someone who wishes to avoid "livesaving" medical treatment such as respiration, nutrition and hydration must make those wishes known by clear and convincing evidence.

There are now two legally-recognized ways an individual can do this—by signing a durable power of attorney for health care or a living will.

Unfortunately, there are disadvantages to both approaches. Few states expressly recognize durable powers of attorney for health care, limiting an attorney-in-fact's powers to supervising financial matters. And only about a dozen states allow people to appoint a proxy to supervise living will wishes. Some states require a verified diagnosis of a terminal illness before either document becomes binding. Most states require that the document be renewed every few years. Some do not allow patients to refuse nutrition and hydration. And all require that the state's own form be used.

The result of all this legal and medical chaos is that experts now advise people to fill out both a power of attorney for health care and a durable power of attorney. But it is difficult enough to get people to overcome psychological barriers and plan for death; requiring two complicated and confusing forms surely impedes the effort.

WHAT TO DO

Those who wish to put their health care wishes in writing should be able to do it by filling out one simple document, a Medical Treatment Statement. This document should be the same in all states and should:

- allow an individual to specify whatever treatment or medication should be administered or denied in case of incapacity;
- remain in effect until specifically revoked or changed;
- be binding on treating physicians, but empower a named family member or friend to make sure all directions are followed; and
- be kept at a single, national office, so that physicians and hospitals could track down the information quickly and efficiently. This nonprofit, computerized system could easily be funded by requiring a slight charge to file or update a Statement. Most people would consider that money well spent for peace of mind for themselves and those close to them.

Individual doctors should be required to discuss the Medical Treatment Statement with patients, and hospitals should make them available as part of their admissions procedures.

The Patient Self-Determination Act passed by Congress in 1990 is a step toward ensuring patients know of their right to direct care. But it is strictly limited to facilities receiving Medicare or Medicaid.

DEFINING THE DOCUMENTS

A durable power of attorney for health care is a document that allows a person to designate a trusted relative or friend as an "attorney-in-fact" to make health care decisions on his or her behalf should the person become unable to do so. The advantage for a struggling or unaware patient is that another human being is authorized to supervise the care.

A living will is a document requiring a doctor to withdraw life-sustaining care, in certain circumstances, if a person later becomes unable to communicate those wishes. About 40 states now legally sanction living wills; about a quarter of them allow appointing a trusted person, called a proxy, to make health care decisions if the patient cannot. The advantage of a living will is that it contractually obligates the doctor to follow a patient's wishes for treatment or to find another doctor who will honor them.

UNTIL THERE'S A BETTER WAY

The Society for the Right To Die, the country's oldest patients' rights organization, tracks legislation and court cases that affect the right to control medical treatment. For a free, up-to-date, state-specific living will form and durable power of attorney for health care form, send your request and a stamped, self-addressed envelope to: The Society for the Right To Die, 250 West 57th Street, Suite 323, New York NY 10107 (212) 246-6973

27 Reform the Jury System

The jury system is inefficient—and mistreats those it calls upon for help. Jurors must make excruciatingly difficult decisions, but are given only garbled legalistic instructions and are strictly prohibited from taking an active part in trials.

More Americans than ever are being called for jury duty. Potential jurors spend most of their time in crowded holding rooms. There they wait for hours, sometimes days, to find out whether judges and attorneys will deign to call them into a courtroom and assess their suitability as jurors. Many never get called. Those who do often wish they hadn't been.

Many of those who are initially called are rejected, but only after attorneys and the judge publicly subject them to intrusive and often irrelevant questioning: Have you ever been raped? Have you ever stolen anything? Have you ever been arrested for drunk driving? Sometimes it seems as if the jury is on trial.

And lawyers often settle cases moments before trial. Having served as unwitting players in the bluffing game between lawyers, many of whom never planned to go trial in the first place, the jurors are told they are no longer needed.

Those picked as jurors face a tough job. Some must evaluate the graphic evidence of a violent crime, which may take a heavy psychological toll. Others must listen to the laborious details of a complicated civil lawsuit, which may try their patience. Many jurors complain about judges' condescending attitudes. Others note that trials drag on days longer than necessary as attorneys pontificate and perform.

Another problem usually surfaces when the evidence is finally in: When they go to deliberate, jurors are often given instructions so laden with legal lingo that they're incomprehensible. If the jury pleads for help during deliberations, judges may refuse, claiming fairness prevents them from explaining away the confusion. So after painstakingly listening to evidence, jurors often end up debating, not the case before them, but the meaning of legal garble.

For doing what they feel is their civic responsibility, those summoned for jury duty are paid chump change—about $7 a day plus token mileage costs in most states. While this makes poor sense in criminal cases, it's an even stronger insult in civil matters, which are typically big dollar personal injury or business cases for which the lawyers charge huge fees.

WHAT TO DO

Jurors must be treated with the respect they deserve.

■ Courts should expand the methods used to locate potential jurors. Most courts now use voter registration lists, taxing the patience of even the most civic-minded, who are called for jury duty after each election. But some courts draw potential jurors from drivers' registration and state income taxation lists—a step in the right direction.

- Courts should adopt a "one day, one trial" system, now in place in a few courtrooms in Connecticut and Massachusetts. Under that approach, a person is called for a day of jury duty and if not assigned to a trial, need not return. If chosen for a trial, however, the juror must serve as long as that trial lasts. More people are called for jury duty, making juries more representative. And it eliminates the long idle waits jurors have when they are on call for several weeks.

- If jurors must be on call for longer than one day before being seated on a jury, they should not have to wait at the courthouse. Some courts now allow jurors to check in at the courthouse by telephone to see whether their services are required. But most require frequent checking, making it impossible to go to work or concentrate for long periods. One telephone check daily should be sufficient.

- Potential jurors should be sifted more efficiently. For example, many of the background questions that often disqualify a person as a juror, such as occupation or family make-up, could be answered in a simple questionnaire, so that those obviously disqualified could be dismissed. Only the more pointed questions on objectivity and bias would be posed and answered in a time-consuming court session.

- Jurors should be paid a decent day's wage. For civil cases, juror pay should be charged to the litigating parties.

- More courts should adopt the process pioneered in Wisconsin and now used in some other states, where jurors are encouraged to question the witnesses. Jurors submit written questions to the trial judge, who discusses each question with the attorneys in private. In the courtroom, the judge reads approved questions to the witnesses. The lawyers can clear up questions that are troubling the jury, and the jurors are more interested and attentive during the trial.

- Finally, all jury instructions should be clear and easy to understand. Accomplishing this should not be hard, since the same written instructions are used repeatedly. Each state should draw up uniform instructions which should pass muster by a Plain English Commission designated to review them.

MANY ARE CALLED

Percentage of adult Americans summoned for jury duty in 1990: 45

Percentage of those summoned in 1984: 35

Percentage of those summoned who actually serve as jurors: 17

Percentage who served as jurors two times or more: 7

EXCUSES, EXCUSES

Percentage of women excused from jury panels: 23

Percentage of men excused: 33

YOU CAN MOVE, BUT YOU CANNOT HIDE

Percentage of people living in the western U.S. called for jury duty: 55

Percentage called in southern states: 51

Percentage called in eastern states: 43

Percentage called in midwest states: 34

Statistics from 1990 survey by Research & Forecasts, New York

Commerce never really flourishes so much, as when it is delivered from the guardianship of legislators and ministers.
—William Godwin
English novelist

28 Help Struggling Businesses

Chapter 11 of the federal bankruptcy law is designed to shelter a struggling business from liquidation while it tries to mend its fiscal ways. In reality, seeking protection under Chapter 11 is a signal for a plague of lawyers to descend. After that, there is seldom any business left to save.

The purpose of the Chapter 11 bankruptcy procedure is to help a debt-beleaguered business keep operating while dealing fairly with its creditors. Congress created it because employees, suppliers, customers and sometimes whole communities have an interest in the recovery of a financially-troubled business.

Once a Chapter 11 bankruptcy is filed, the bankruptcy court appoints a trustee to take over or supervise the business while a reorganization plan is developed for the court to approve. Often the trustee is the business's chief executive or other officer. But if the managers appear unable to cope with the problem, an outside trustee is brought in.

During this interim period, secured creditors are given an important voice in how the business operates and must agree to the reorganization plan before the court will approve it. Unsecured creditors and stockholders can also have significant input.

Typically, unsecured creditors of the business agree to be paid a percentage of what they are owed. Secured creditors—creditors who have liens on business assets as security for loans or credit—also accept less rigorous repayment terms than they originally required. In exchange for these concessions, the business is usually required to alter and improve its operations.

But standing next to every major creditor is a high-priced attorney. The troubled business and its chief executive officer serving as trustee also hire lawyers to represent them in the proceedings. If an independent trustee is appointed to manage the business, add two lawyers—the trustee, who is usually a lawyer, and a lawyer to represent the trustee in bankruptcy court. In short, depending on the size of the business and the number of creditors, there may be dozens of attorneys involved in a Chapter 11 case.

The more lawyers involved in a case, the longer it takes and the more it costs. Court hearings, depositions and negotiations all represent lots of billable time for bankruptcy lawyers who charge $200 an hour. One two-hour meeting with ten lawyers present puts a $4,000 dent in the business's coffers, without counting time to prepare.

Not only does the bankrupt business pay all legal fees, but lawyers get paid before other creditors. Bankruptcy judges—who are usually ex-bankruptcy attorneys—have the power to limit the fees, but they seldom do.

The result of the Chapter 11 approach is predictably disastrous: Very few businesses ever produce a viable reorganization plan. After a year or two of profuse bleeding by lawyers, most are forced to liquidate and are never heard from again. Their creditors, employees and communities all lose.

WHAT TO DO

The Chapter 11 bankruptcy system should be scrapped and replaced by a federal business reorganization agency with regional offices in major cities. Any business unable to work things out with its creditors should be able to apply for advice and help. After a business filed for protection, creditors would temporarily be barred from trying to collect debts from the business.

The agency would quickly examine the business's books, talk to managers and creditors, and decide whether the business was a likely candidate for successful reorganization. If the agency concluded the business couldn't be saved, it would immediately be placed into Chapter 7 (straight liquidation) bankruptcy, where its assets would be divided among creditors. A business owner who disagreed with this assessment would have the right to a fast and fair appeal.

If it looked as if the business could be saved, the agency would work with the business to formulate a plan to keep it going and pay creditors all or a portion of the debts over a reasonable period. No attorneys would be involved in drawing up or implementing the plan. Creditors who refused to go along with the proposed reorganization plan would be paid a partial amount of what they were owed, based on the agency's assessment of the business's assets and liabilities. Since this is almost always far less than the face value of the debt, it would behoove most creditors to wait and hope the business returned to solvency.

THE CHAPTER 11 TRAP: A CASE STUDY

Sol Stein, former owner of the prestigious publishing house of Stein and Day, has written a blow-by-blow account of how the Chapter 11 process destroyed his vulnerable business. In it, he explains why only lawyers benefit from the system:

"In the real world one earns one's keep by having a productive day. Not so in Chapter 11, because its participants are chiefly lawyers doing time. That is, they are being measured by their firms for the billing hours served and not by what they actually accomplish for the client."

Stein also quotes an honest lawyer on mendacity in Chapter 11 proceedings: "The players speak words like *God, country, fiduciary responsibility,* and *equity,* the collective meaning of which, absent the doubletalk, boils down to *my fee, my fee.*"

—From *A Feast for Lawyers*
M. Evans and Co. 1990

It's a lot cheaper to buy a judge than a governor or an entire legislature and he can probably do a lot more for you.
—Leslie Jacobs
Former president of the
Ohio Bar Association

29 Abolish Judicial Elections

Many elected judges owe their jobs to the political parties that nominate them and the lawyers who finance their campaigns. When the lawyers who make hefty contributions appear before those judges, or a case comes before them that involves other party faithful, suspicion is cast on the judges' ability to be fair.

Forty states hold judicial elections. In some of those states, judges compete in partisan elections, just like other officeholders. In others, after judges are elected or appointed, they must periodically run for retention. They don't have opponents, but must receive a certain percentage of the vote—commonly, about 60%—to keep their jobs.

To get elected, judges must raise money for their campaigns. In an urban area, even a local race for a trial court judgeship can cost up to $100,000. And millions of dollars are spent in high-profile state supreme court elections.

Overwhelmingly, the money needed to wage successful campaigns comes from lawyers. Contributions seem intended more to curry favor than to ensure that high-quality candidates are elected. Unopposed candidates often receive more contributions than judges in contested races, according to a recent three-year study in Cook County, Illinois. Some lawyers, just to be on the safe side, contribute to *both* candidates in a judicial election, or to judges who aren't even up for election. In some states, judicial candidates are free to keep excess campaign funds after the election, so some contributions are little more than indirect cash payments.

And judges usually know just who donated how much, even if the gifts are made to a campaign committee that technically is a separate entity. The names of people who contribute more than a small amount are in most places a matter of public record. Ironically, this attempt to clean up campaigns by revealing who financed them made matters worse. One California judge, now retired, was notorious for keeping the list of lawyer-contributors under his desk blotter in court. When a lawyer asked for some special consideration for a client, the judge would slowly lift the corner of the blotter and peer at the list before announcing his decision.

Lawyers' contributions to judicial races have reached appalling proportions. During the multi-billion dollar 1980s litigation between Pennzoil and Texaco in Texas, for example, Pennzoil lawyers donated more than $315,000 to state supreme court justices. Some of the money went to three justices who weren't even running for office. Texaco lawyers gave $72,000 to five supreme court justices. Pennzoil eventually won.

Proponents of choosing judges by election say that elections force judges to be accountable to voters. But elected judges may end up more accountable to a small pool of heavy contributors than to voters. And popular political pressure may actually interfere with judges' performance of their duties, because they must sometimes take unpopular stands to decide cases fairly.

Elections leave judges beholden not only to lawyer-contributors but also, in states where political parties nominate judicial candidates, to their party. Once on the bench, they can be expected to be both grateful for the previous election and fearful of the next one. If another public officeholder from the same party is involved or interested in a case, the judge's political connections may raise the question of possible bias.

As Thomas Phillips, Chief Justice of the Texas Supreme Court, has pointed out, "What makes a good judge isn't anything an election brings out very well." Judicial elections are "infused with party politics," concluded the New York State Commission on Government Integrity in 1988. The commission, which had been created by New York Governor Mario Cuomo, recommended that all judges be appointed. Cuomo has repeatedly proposed amending the state's constitution to allow a judicial appointment system (most

New York judges are now elected), but both Democratic and Republican party leaders have strongly resisted, fearing the loss of political influence and patronage.

WHAT TO DO

As long as there are judicial elections of any kind, judges should at least be required to excuse themselves from cases in which contributing lawyers or clients appear. That would act as the surest deterrent to contributions that may affect judges' impartiality.

But it's time to end the practice of electing judges, so that judges don't owe their jobs to money and favor from lawyers or political parties—both of whom may expect some future benefits from their investments.

Replacing elections with a truly non-political and open process is difficult. Any new system should avoid the shortcomings of some attempts at so-called "merit selection" of judges, which are far from non-political. When a governor or legislature is given authority to appoint judges, for example, the power becomes just another form of patronage, and political connections are still rewarded. Texas lawyer Mack Kidd, an opponent of merit selection, was credited with the observation: "At least under the elective system, if someone tries to buy a judgeship it's out in the open."

A better system would be to give the job of choosing judges to a nonpartisan screening committee made up of judges and other citizens. The criteria used to evaluate judicial candidates should be non-political: experience, temperament and knowledge. Judges selected in this way would not owe their jobs to either political parties or to lawyers who argue cases before them.

Forty-seven percent of all the written responses to taxpayers are incorrect. How can we even contemplate prosecuting anybody?

—U.S. Rep. Christopher Shays

30 Remove the Rust from the IRS

Few things fill us with greater dread than receiving an envelope bearing the return address of the Internal Revenue Service. There is increasing cause for alarm. The powerful IRS, responsible for collecting more than 90% of the federal government's trillion-dollar budget, is increasingly slow, inefficient— and wrong.

Nearly every year, the IRS claims it has finally simplified tax forms, even dubbing one the EZ form. But it's taxing just to read the instructions, like this one in the popular Application for Extension of Time To File:

When to file. *The application for extension of time to file must be submitted on or before the due date of the return or the extended due date if you file for an Additional extension of time after you have previously filed an Automatic 4-month extension of time application. The application should be submitted in sufficient time to enable processing by the Department of Finance and Revenue.*

The IRS also claims to provide help over a convenient Taxpayer Assistance telephone hotline. But taxpayers report that it is well-nigh impossible to get through around tax time. Those who finally get past the long-holding recording are often steered wrong. IRS officials reported in 1989 that while the rate of accurate responses given on its hotline

had increased, more than one out of four callers was misinformed.

However, in hunting down those who owe money, the 120,000-person IRS bureaucracy is more effective. The IRS estimates that taxpayers shortchange the government $80 to $100 billion each year by not filing returns, underreporting income and overstating deductions. Another $90 billion remains due from those who admit they owe but cannot pay.

Doggedly going after the cheaters, in 1990, the IRS notified nearly 36 million individuals that they owed more in taxes and penalties. The top four failings, according to the IRS, were: math errors; returns filed late; misreported income, interest or dividends; and miscalculated quarterly payments.

But lest we all rest assured that the IRS is doing its job, heed the startlingly different picture revealed in a 1990 Gallup poll commissioned by *Money* magazine. Of those who contested the tax due notices sent by the IRS, 45% reported the IRS claims were completely erroneous; an additional 24% said the agency was partially wrong. Of those who challenged the IRS, 53% wound up paying nothing, and another 17% paid a greatly reduced sum.

Despite this evidence that the IRS is so fuddled that it often goes after the wrong people for the wrong amounts, most people challenged by the IRS simply pay up and shut up. Those who fight back often wish they hadn't, as the IRS red tape quickly ensnares them. This includes a series of progressively ominous letters from the IRS; the last arrives by certified mail and threatens that the federal government will clamp a lien on the taxpayer's property if the contested tax is not paid promptly.

Compounding the fear created by the IRS' liberally applied scare tactics is a greater fear: Most taxpayers have no idea how to be sure that they are right. Tax laws are difficult to master, and they change yearly. Of course, professional help is available, but it is forbiddingly expensive. And even if the taxpayer is plainly right, proving that to the IRS typically requires a great deal of tenacity and a good many organized records and receipts. It often costs more money and energy to demonstrate that the IRS is wrong than to pay it money you may not owe.

WHAT TO DO

In the long run, people are more likely to pay taxes when they understand what they owe and feel the collection process is fair. Here is how the IRS can meet these simple goals:

- Make tax forms simple to fill out by rewriting them in clear language, providing concise instructions.

- Give accurate assistance to taxpayers who need more information. Taxpayer assistance phone lines should be adequately staffed by trained personnel so that taxpayers not only are able to reach help, but are given correct information when they do.

- Make it practical to file returns electronically. The IRS instituted the procedure a few years ago, but put many restrictions on how it could be done—requiring those who wished to file electronically to pay for a special IRS-approved transmitter. Some larger tax preparation offices have the transmitters—but they are out of cost-range for most individuals. To save time, paper and transcription errors, transmitters should be made available for taxpayers at a number of convenient, public locales such as post offices.

A HESITANT STEP IN THE RIGHT DIRECTION, MAYBE?

The IRS has set up the Problem Resolution Program (PRP), a go-between service for taxpayers and the IRS to resolve problems. The 300 PRP offices nationwide handle taxpayer complaints from smoothing out discrepancies in state returns to delaying the time the IRS will seize property to satisfy back taxes.

But the program has two big drawbacks: Few people know it exists. And taxpayers must first run head-on into the IRS bureaucracy. PRPs help only those who have received at least three complaint letters from the IRS or who have been treated rudely by IRS personnel. And a taxpayer must first have made at least two attempts to clear up the problem by calling the local tax office or the number listed on the IRS letter. PRPs will not help interpret tax laws; they will assist only in cutting through the IRS's red tape.

Contact the national PRP office at (202) 566-6475. Or call the toll-free number, 800-424-1040, to find the nearest branch office.

31 Bring Competition to the Law Business

Lawyers have long enjoyed a monopoly in selling legal information and services. The result is excessive fees for those who can pay—and no legal help for those who cannot.

It is well-accepted that monopolies of all kinds cause higher prices, lower quality services and large-scale inefficiencies. Because they are so destructive to our economy and freedom, most monopolies are illegal. So too, many argue, is the monopoly of the lawyer cartel, a loose association of individual lawyers, law firms and state and local bar associations which together orchestrate unwritten policies that work to fix prices and stamp out competition.

Lawyers jealously guard their monopoly over providing legal services by enforcing state laws and court rules making it illegal for anyone but licensed lawyers to practice law. To this day, non-lawyers can be, and occasionally are, sent to jail for violating these laws and rules. Most often, however, judges simply order the non-lawyer competitor out of business.

Appallingly, these lawyer-written laws almost never define the key phrase "practice of law." Instead, judges decide whether specific behavior called to their attention should be punished for infringing on the legal profession's turf. Not a bad deal from the

lawyers' point of view: They get to make and enforce the rules as they go along.

Sadly, despite the probable illegality of the lawyer cartel's efforts to prevent competition, ultimate enforcement of the anti-monopoly laws must come from judges. But judges are also lawyers. They are not only long-term economic beneficiaries of the cartel's practices, but also the recipients of a lifetime of brainwashing from law schools and professional organizations about the monopoly's virtues. So the lawyer cartel continues untouched by judicial intervention.

And when it comes to non-lawyers' right to represent people in courts, judges sit even more firmly in the driver's seat. Asserting their constitutional authority to regulate who appears before them as advocates, courts ban all but lawyers, even though many agree with Warren Burger, former Chief Justice of the U.S. Supreme Court, that lots of lawyers are incompetent.

Disgusting as it is for lawyers to abuse the legal system by shutting down and even jailing their competitors, the cartel's real victims are the millions of Americans who are priced out of the legal system. Even the American Bar Association laments that as many as one hundred million Americans cannot afford fundamental legal help. Yet the ABA and its affiliate state bar associations are unwilling to seriously entertain any solution that doesn't let the legal profession continue to limit competition.

WHAT TO DO

Laws and court rules that prohibit practicing law without a license should be repealed, making non-lawyers free to provide basic legal services, including form preparation for divorces, bankruptcies, probates and most other routine uncontested actions. Consumers, not lawyers, should be allowed to decide who to turn to for legal help.

In most states, repeal of authorized practice laws must come from state legislatures, which, although often dominated by lawyers, are ultimately accountable to the public. In a few states where measures with enough grassroots support can be put right on the ballot, interested consumers could push for this legislation directly.

This new deregulated system would benefit lawyers as well as consumers. Lawyers would shift from low-skill legal tasks, such as handling uncontested probates, guardianships or divorces to areas involving more technical knowledge, much as doctors have turned the task of taking peoples' temperature and blood pressure and running diagnostic machines over to others.

In this deregulated environment, the public must be protected from dishonest or incompetent providers. Everyone who provides legal services—lawyers and non-lawyers alike—should be required to register with a state agency, prominently display their educational qualifications and experience. In legal areas where the public would be put at risk by incompetent work, all providers should be required to pass a skills-based examination.

THE LAW STORE

Deregulating the legal services business would allow law stores, on the order of H & R Block tax preparation offices, to open on every corner.

The typical law store, staffed by both lawyers and non-lawyers, would offer consumers a range of legal services. It would sell self-help law books, software and audio and videotapes. It would also provide access to a coin-operated, user-friendly computer connected to a legal database so that people could look up information.

Typists would charge by the page for completing legal documents prepared by customers using self-help law materials. Non-lawyers trained in specific legal subject areas, such as family law or bankruptcy, would provide information and prepare forms for customers who were willing to pay higher fees for it. Attorneys would offer legal diagnosis, consultations on especially knotty issues and representation in court.

If law school graduates, like cars, could be recalled for failure to meet commercial standards, the recall rate would be very high on those who go into courts without substantial added training.

—Warren Burger
Former Chief Justice of
the U.S. Supreme Court

32 Restrict Lawyers' Licenses

A license to practice law is no guarantee of legal knowledge, skill or experience in a particular area. Incompetent lawyers regularly mislead and defraud clients who rely on the lawyer label.

For the steep fees they pay, people who go to lawyers expect first-class legal knowledge and expertise. But as many clients discover, someone who has a license to practice law may not know the nuts and bolts of a particular legal area. Even worse, some clients never discover that they got faulty advice or representation and that shoddy lawyering may have cost them important rights—and their savings.

According to state bar associations—the lawyers' groups who hand out law licenses—aspiring lawyers undergo rigorous training and pass a tough exam before being loosed on the public. All this preparation is one of the prime justifications for the current lawyer monopoly on providing legal services. Only these specially-trained people, according to the bar, can cope with the complexities of our legal system.

In fact, most law schools teach little of how the law actually works, or how to deal with clients or courts. Instead, schools concentrate on the decisions of appeals courts and legal history and theory. But all that bears little relation to why most people hire lawyers.

People need lawyers who can consult the relevant laws, advise on possible courses of action and prepare the right paperwork.

The bar exam is even more out of touch. The day-to-day skills lawyers are commonly believed to possess—research, writing, counseling clients, dealing with courts, mastering a wide variety of basic legal concepts—are not tested. Fledgling lawyers are expected to pick up these skills after they have their licenses—giving a disturbing meaning to the expression "practicing law."

Once past the bar exam, lawyers are never tested again. Some states require lawyers to take continuing education classes, but these requirements are minimal. Lawyers may even get credit for watching videotapes on law office management.

But what is most outrageous about licenses to practice law is their breadth. They give lawyers the right to take on any kind of case, from divorce to murder to probate to zoning. Any lawyer is free to list any number of "specialties" in a yellow pages ad or on a business card, even if he or she has no experience in that area of law.

WHAT TO DO

Lawyers' licenses should be limited to certain subject areas—family law, criminal law, tax or probate, for example. A separate exam would be given for each specialty. That way, an exam could test the skills and knowledge needed by a lawyer who wants to represent clients in a particular legal subject area.

Like pilots who must have a license for each type of aircraft they want to fly, law school graduates could take as many of the exams and amass as many of the limited licenses as they wanted. People looking to hire a lawyer would have a much better idea of what kind of expertise they were getting.

Several other reforms would complement this fundamental change in lawyer licensing:

■ Law schools should offer more practical courses, including trial practice, client counseling and other subjects that directly pertain to law practice.

■ Before new lawyers are licensed and turned out into the community, they should be required to serve a one-year apprenticeship in a specialty they have chosen. Doctors fresh out of medical school undergo years of hands-on training; a comparable system could greatly improve the legal profession.

Such a program should not merely supply cheap labor for law firms. It must require structured supervision from a lawyer who has a license in the specialty and experience in specific, practical areas of the field. After the apprenticeship period, the new lawyer would be eligible to take the exam to get a license in that specialty.

■ Testing on substantive law and procedure should continue as long as a lawyer practices. As it is, people are periodically retested before renewing their driver's licenses, but a lawyer's license is good for life. It is taken away only for the worst misconduct. Simple incompetence, including failure to keep current on the always-changing law, is never reason enough, unfortunately.

33 Make Traffic Court Fair

People who want to fight an unfair traffic ticket commonly are kept ignorant of their rights and must overcome insulting and unnecessary bureaucratic obstacles. When they finally get to court, they are typically presumed to be lying and are almost automatically found guilty.

Going to traffic court could be a valuable lesson in civics—a chance to have the satisfaction of getting one's day in court before an impartial judge. Instead, people encounter a bureaucratic maze designed to discourage them from fighting their tickets. Those who persist too often find their cases heard in a kangaroo court atmosphere, in which they're guilty until they prove themselves innocent.

Typically, someone who receives a traffic citation must trek to the courthouse and wait in a long line to get an appointment. Weeks or even months later, the traffic offender must again journey to court—only to say the words "not guilty" at an arraignment. Then the judge sets a trial date a few more weeks or months away. To add further insult to the inconvenience, in many places, a citizen must pay the fine (post bail) before the trial date.

When the trial day finally arrives, things usually get worse—especially for a busy person who has had to take off from work. For starters, there is likely to be a long wait. When the case is finally called, the judge will probably accept the officer's statement of what happened without question—while barely listening to any other version. In some courts, judges even refuse to look at pictures or diagrams offered by defendants, or listen to their legal arguments if they aren't represented by lawyers. In short, no matter how strong a case, there is an overwhelming likelihood that someone accused of a traffic violation will be found guilty.

In the age of "no new taxes," politicians desperate to balance the books have lost sight of the purpose of traffic laws—to discourage unsafe driving—and view them instead as a way to bring in money. Because many people wisely conclude that it's easier to pay a fine than to put in time standing in line on three different days just to get an unfair trial, the government has a sure moneymaker by keeping things the way they are.

If this all sounds like a conspiracy, there's good reason. To understand it, you need only look at how the large revenues generated by traffic court fines are divvied up. A typical state might operate like this: First, there's a "penalty assessment" over and above the amount of the ticket; that goes for courthouse and jail construction. Then, the city whose officer gave the ticket gets a cut. Much of this money, sometimes a fixed percentage, goes directly to the police department's budget. Next, the courts get a percentage. In some places, traffic court revenues are used to pay judges or fund pension plans.

It's not only greed that causes traffic court judges to side with police officers in court:

The judges must run for re-election regularly. To keep their jobs, they usually want the influential support of the local police officers' association. One good way to get this support is to side with police officers in traffic cases most of the time.

WHAT TO DO

Traffic court should treat people fairly and efficiently at the same time that it deters unsafe driving. Here's how:

- Sever the connection between traffic fines and courthouse and police funding. A good place to put the money would be to fund traffic safety programs.

- Include basic instructions on how people can assert their rights to a fair hearing on an information sheet handed out with the ticket. Back this up with a courthouse voice mail system which routes information requests to recorded messages or, if necessary, someone who can answer questions.

- Allow people to enter not guilty pleas and arrange court appearances by mail or phone.

- Schedule court appearances at convenient hours, including Saturdays and evenings.

- Train and retrain commissioners and judges who hear traffic court cases to scrupulously try to find the truth, and not just rely on the police officer's story.

- Take politics out of traffic court. Cases should be heard by appointed commissioners who can judge on the merits, not with half their attention on the next election.

So long as little children are allowed to suffer, there is no true love in the world.
—Isadora Duncan

34 Reform the Child Support System

About 25% of American children now live in poverty. Many of them are in families headed by single parents, dependent upon support from the other parent. But, too often, court-ordered support isn't paid—a problem made worse by inefficient and costly collection bureaucracies operated by the states.

When parents split up, one of them—most often the mother—gets physical custody of the children. The other parent becomes obligated to pay child support. In some instances, the support payments are enough, when added to the other income, to provide the children with a decent life. But more often, the actual contributions are far too little.

Whether adequate child support is paid depends on both the efficiency of the enforcement effort and the responsible parent's health, attitude, employment and other financial obligations, including the need to support a second family. Severe restrictions on visitation rights, whether justified or not, often cause a parent to hold back support payments.

A good many parents, despite any number of court orders and stringent enforcement efforts, will not pay any support for their children. They are unemployed, chronic drug and alcohol abusers—or out of touch and impossible to track down. And under the current legal system, their children get nothing; they are the innocent victims of circumstance.

Even when court-ordered support obligations are fully paid, they are often less than dependent children need. When a mother has custody, her ability to make up the difference is often limited by a variety of factors, including the time she must spend nurturing the children, lack of affordable high-quality child care and the wage structure of a marketplace that discriminates against women and devalues jobs they have traditionally held.

Underpaid and unpaid child support have not escaped the attention of federal and state governments. Annually, they pay billions of welfare dollars to single-parent families. And billions more go to large bureaucracies that hound parents who don't meet their obligations. New federal laws require states to enact mandatory levels of child support that will be uniformly applied by judges statewide. States are also required to implement tough collection measures, including collecting support through automatic paycheck deductions.

These may sound like radical steps in the right direction, but there are several major problems with these enforcement efforts. The most glaring is that the amount spent on collection efforts often equals or surpasses the amount collected. According to a 1988 report to Congress, 19 states spent more than they collected in 1987. For instance, Alaska fell short of its administrative costs by 25%, while Arizona spent almost twice as much as it recovered. This waste of money is often the result of mindless government efforts to squeeze payments from those who can't pay.

The current system also puts one parent in the role of bill collector and paints the other as a permanent debtor. Predictably, hassles over late payments and less than full payments contribute to future child support delinquencies. This is especially true if custody or visitation arrangements are in dispute.

In addition, most methods aimed at enforcing support payments rely heavily on seizing a portion of a parent's wages. But other forms of income such as royalties, commissions and accounts receivable often are not touched, allowing some parents—including some relatively wealthy ones—to escape their support obligations.

WHAT TO DO

The current system of enforcing support obligations should be scrapped, and a new federal system for collecting and distributing child support should be substituted. The new system should be guided by two simple principles. First, all children, regardless of their parents' income, should receive at least the minimum level of support to keep them out of poverty. And second, all parents should contribute to their children's support. Money to pay for supplementary support for children whose parents can't provide the minimum acceptable amount could come from the billions of dollars made available by a tough and efficient new collection system.

The new collection system should look like this:

- All child support awards set by local courts would conform to national minimum needs standards.
- All support orders would be registered with the Internal Revenue Service, which would collect the payments—either directly from paychecks or through quarterly estimated child support contribution returns—and deposit them into a Children's Support Fund.
- Random audits focusing on the self-employed and others who receive from sources other than conventional employment would bring in millions of dollars that currently isn't collected.
- The inefficient state-run child support collection bureaucracies would be closed down, and the state and federal money slated each year to fund them would go into the Children's Support Fund.

The new disbursement system should look like this:

- Child support checks would be mailed monthly, as Social Security checks are now.
- Children would receive all money contributed by their parents.
- If a child's parent contributed less than the federal minimum needs standard, the child would receive a supplemental amount from the general Fund large enough to reach that standard.

35 Compensate Medical Malpractice Victims

Victims of medical malpractice are injured twice: first by faulty medicine, then by a fatuously slow legal system that requires them to prove who caused their injuries. And because a few who win get unrealistically high awards, health insurance costs rise for everyone, and doctors are scared into practicing costly "defensive medicine."

Fewer than five percent of the people injured while under medical care receive any compensation. To win a lawsuit, a victim must prove who caused the injury—an extremely difficult task given the complexities of modern medicine and the common reaction of doctors, which is to cover up their mistakes.

A 1990 study of 33,000 New York hospital patients showed that nearly 1,400 of them suffered harm beyond the expected risks of their treatment—injuries that totaled $895 million in medical bills and lost wages. But only one in four could trace the injury to some person's careless act.

If an injured person takes a malpractice case to trial, everyone has a motive to lie. The lawyer must win to get paid—and the bigger the amount that the jury awards, the bigger the lawyer's fee. The doctor fears a damaged reputation and still higher malpractice insurance rates.

The jurors must decide who is the lesser liar and must sort through complex technical testimony and difficult issues about who was legally at fault. It's no wonder that they sometimes respond viscerally to the injured victim's plight and vote to compensate that person from the thickest available wallet.

Yet, primarily because patients have a difficult time figuring out and proving who caused their injuries, the majority of those who do sue for malpractice do not fare well; only 20% win. And they wait an average of seven years before getting a penny. Much of the amount awarded by a jury—commonly, 30 to 40%—goes to pay the lawyers.

Even though most malpractice victims are shortchanged, the health care system is choking on the cost of these lawsuits. Annual malpractice insurance premiums have shot up, some into the six-figure range. This contributes to the big medical bills that in turn make health insurance unaffordable for millions.

Lawyers contend that the medical profession needs the threat of huge jury awards as an incentive to police itself. Yet the fear of legal liability has seriously damaged the quality of medical care Americans receive. Doctors who are justifiably afraid of lawsuits may cover up for each other when mistakes are made.

Doctors' fear of malpractice awards also results in bad medical care. Both overtesting and overtreating are standard cover-your-tail methods of beating malpractice suits. The result: The U.S. has the highest rate of

Caesarean sections in the world, tens of thousands of unneeded surgeries are performed each year and expensive technology is regularly misused—CAT scans to diagnose simple headaches, for example.

Paradoxically, some doctors also try to avoid liability by undertreating. Because new procedures carry a higher risk of harm and of second-guessing later, doctors often stick to conventional treatments, even in terminal cases, for fear of lawsuits alleging that the advanced treatment hastened the patient's death. The American Cancer Society estimated in 1986 that 10,000 cancer patients a year die as a result.

WHAT TO DO

We should adopt a no-fault method to compensate all patients injured while under medical care. The system should:

- quickly compensate all who have suffered harm as a result of medical treatment, regardless of how it occurred;

- give doctors incentives to root out and expose the causes of medical error;
- base a victim's economic recovery on actual economic loss—medical costs, loss of income and disability—plus, where there is long-term or permanent disability, a reasonable amount for lost quality of life; and
- handle compensation administratively through a state-run Injured Patients Board, which could track information with a beefed-up Medical Board that monitors doctors.

A no-fault insurance system that would compensate all medical malpractice victims for economic loss would be expensive to administer. Fortunately, however, no-fault would cost no more than doctors and hospitals now spend on inflated malpractice insurance premiums each year—much of which ultimately goes to pay lawyers. Real savings would also result from the substantial reduction of overtreatment and unnecessary operations.

THE INSURANCE INDUSTRY: A PARTNER IN THE CRIME

The insurance industry is as much to blame for the current crisis as is the legal system. While crying poor for the last 15 years and blaming it on vast jury awards and a lawsuit-happy society, insurers have in fact made big bucks. Consider these facts recently uncovered by the General Accounting Office:

- Only state agencies oversee the industry; it is exempt from both antitrust laws and the Federal Trade Commission.
- Insurers made $2.2 billion in profits from malpractice insurance between 1975 and 1985.
- Half of all malpractice claims are unsettled five years after they have been claimed. During this time insurers report the claims as losses, while earning lots of money owed the claimants. Until the Tax Reform Act of 1986, insurers were using this dubious method of accounting to avoid paying millions of dollars in taxes.
- The insurance industry routinely underreports its rate of return on investments and overstates inflation when requesting rate hikes. And it gets them.
- Half of all personal bankruptcies in the U.S. in a given year are the result of unexpected illness.
- One million families in 1982 were refused health care because they lacked insurance.

*Perfect freedom is as necessary to the
health and vigor of commerce, as it is to
the health and vigor of citizenship.*
—Patrick Henry

36 Free Small Businesses from the Securities Laws

New corporations and existing ones searching for investors are being strangled in a snarl of securities laws, regulations and red tape. They must complete mountains of complicated legal and financial disclosure paperwork, most of which does little to protect investors from unscrupulous promoters. What it does is divert money to lawyers and accountants.

America depends on small, privately-held businesses to provide innovative goods and services and create new jobs. This benefit of more jobs is particularly significant in today's volatile economy, when automation and overseas plants are replacing more and more domestic manufacturing jobs and many publicly-held corporations are merging and eliminating middle management positions.

Of course, finding people willing to invest in the uncertain prospects of new business can be difficult. Unfortunately, federal and state securities laws make this task even tougher, requiring a complicated and costly ritual of paperwork and procedures before outside investment capital can be solicited. For example, you cannot simply call potential investors—even friends or relatives—to see if they are interested in putting money in your small corporation. First you must comply with the federal securities laws and the securities statutes of your state and the home state of each person contacted.

Soliciting funds from the public is particularly burdensome. It involves filing a stock offering registration with federal and state agencies, preparing disclosure documents and stock offering materials for potential investors, and preparing complicated financial statements. The price tag in accounting and legal fees to generate this paperwork can easily be tens of thousands of dollars.

If you limit your stock offering to a close circle of business associates, friends and relatives or if you seek to raise only a modest amount of money, you may be able to qualify for federal and state exemptions from a full registration of your stock offering.

Although this will save you some time and money and avoid some of the pitfalls of a public offering, you still face a difficult and costly task. These exemptions are highly technical, vary significantly in their requirements, and often require preparing disclosure documents and filing notification forms with state and federal agencies.

The result for most small businesses, whether they qualify for a securities exemption or not, is a series of consultations with a lawyer and an accountant before accepting any funds from outsiders—and inevitably, a hefty bill for services rendered.

It is difficult to justify subjecting small businesses to this sort of procedural overkill. After all, the most unsophisticated consumer can invest a lifetime's savings in a speculative stock issue or commodities investment in the course of a telephone conversation with a stockbroker. The law requires no individual formalities or disclosures.

And the special securities disclosure paperwork rarely leads to any discoveries or second thoughts by prospective investors.

The legal language in these forms is so technical that it is unintelligible to the average investor. And, of course, financial disclosure data can easily be exaggerated by unscrupulous entrepreneurs to overstate the financial prospects of any venture.

Most states and the federal government have special rules that apply to corporate "promoters"—people who help obtain money, property, personnel and whatever else it takes to get a new business up and running. The laws require promoters to disclose facts to all investors in all securities transactions and fill out reams of additional legalese-laden forms. These formalities add nothing but frustration to the small business startup. They have no practical legal effect.

WHAT TO DO

Small business owners should be free to raise startup or expansion money privately from friends, family and others without complicated disclosure procedures or securities filings. The hundreds of nitpicky federal and state regulations should be replaced by one simple one. It should exempt all securities transactions involving private companies and individual investors. As long as the investment funds are put to the uses for which they were solicited, investors should be able to assume the risks of the investment by signing a plain statement to this effect on a standard disclosure form.

This new disclosure form would be used to register the sales of the securities under this exemption and would be filed with a central agency, such as the federal Securities Exchange Commission. The exemption form should be simple and comprehensible. No one should need an accountant or lawyer to make sense of it. An example of such a statement is shown below.

Investors could still be protected against dishonest business promoters by the federal and state securities laws that deal specifically with misrepresentation and fraud.

A PRIVATE INVESTOR DISCLOSURE STATEMENT

I UNDERSTAND THAT THIS IS AN UNCERTAIN AND RISKY INVESTMENT. DESPITE ANY ASSURANCES OR EXPECTATIONS TO THE CONTRARY, I UNDERSTAND THAT I MAY NOT RECEIVE A RETURN ON THIS INVESTMENT AND MAY, IN FACT, LOSE ALL OF THE FUNDS INVESTED. I UNDERSTAND AND ASSUME THESE RISKS.

No guilty man is ever acquitted at the bar
of his own conscience.

—Juvenal

37 Discipline Lawyers

When lawyers mishandle a case or steal a client's money, it is the client who pays and pays again—in fees and in lost legal rights. Those who complain about shoddy service from their lawyers are relegated to a lawyer-run discipline system that protects the profession, not the public.

A growing number of outraged clients are filing complaints against their lawyers, but over 90% of those complaints are dismissed—without investigation.

A glance at the system explains why. The complaints are filed with state bar associations, lawyers' trade groups, which are responsible for monitoring and disciplining their own members. The discipline panels are made up primarily of local lawyers. Injured and angry clients are left unsatisfied, uncompensated and often without the time or energy to fix their original legal problem.

The most common complaint is fee-gouging. Lawyer discipline officials are cavalier, referring complaints to local bar groups. After cursory consideration, they usually conclude that "the reasonable cost" of a lawyer's services is a high one; clients simply must bear it.

The other widespread client complaint against lawyers is that they are incompetent. But unbelievably, incompetence is not considered a reason to discipline lawyers in most states, so these complaints are simply dismissed.

Lawyer discipline proceedings are so biased towards the profession that only three percent of all complaints lead to public pun-

ishment, and most so-called penalties amount to little more than the lawyer promising not to be bad in the future.

The punishment for the few extremely wayward lawyers, typically, is a reprimand or temporary suspension from practice. Less than 10% of cases result in permanent suspension, called disbarment. Even in such cases, a "permanently" suspended lawyer can most often successfully lobby and be readmitted to practice within a few years.

Lawyers almost always discipline other lawyers in secret. This supports the public assumption that hearings are mere meetings of cronies. In most states, the fact that a complaint—or two dozen complaints—have been filed against a lawyer is not made public. Similarly, even information so damaging that it leads to a lawyer being disciplined is kept secret. While this system works admirably to cover up the sins of lawyers, it does nothing to alert unwitting members of the public of the existence of lousy lawyers.

Persistent complainers are told to resort to court and file a malpractice claim against the shoddy lawyer. But most will be hard-pressed to find a lawyer who will sue another lawyer.

While not many get satisfaction, more former clients each year are lodging complaints with the bar associations against their former attorneys: about 70,000 nationwide in 1985, 93,000 in 1988.

To muffle this mounting public outcry, a few state bars have taken hesitant steps to reform their lawyer discipline systems. In 1989, Illinois opened disciplinary hearings to the public for the first time and added a number of non-lawyers to the committee responsible for hearing complaints. Also that year, the number of California lawyers disciplined jumped 44% when the state bar upped its discipline budget 75%, adding a full-time court to hear discipline complaints.

WHAT TO DO

The current system that excludes consumers and leaves lawyers with the impossible task of policing themselves must be replaced by a public, accessible, fast system that resolves a wide range of consumer complaints against lawyers.

Lawyer discipline should be put in the hands of independent state regulatory agencies composed primarily of non-lawyers. These agencies should have the power to investigate lawyers—by conducting random audits of lawyers' trust accounts, for example—not just wait for complaints to come to them. Complaints against lawyers should be evaluated just as other consumer prob-

lems, such as auto or home repair complaints. Remedies should compensate wronged clients and protect them from further injury by punishing wrongdoing lawyers. Here are some specifics:

- Disputes over fees should be evaluated and mediated by independent boards with power to order refunds for overcharging.

- Complaints against lawyers and the results of any official investigations should be easily available to the public.

- Lawyers who have stolen a client's money should be forever prevented from practicing law and prosecuted like other thieves.

- Lawyers who are found to be incompetent should be weeded out quickly and then suspended permanently if their incompetence caused substantial harm. Or, they could be temporarily suspended and required to pass a tough proficiency exam before being allowed to practice law again.

- Clients should be compensated for losses they suffer from incompetent lawyering, including money for out-of-pocket losses. If the lawyer who causes the problem can't pay, provide compensation through a state fund, with the necessary money raised by taxing all practicing lawyers.

LEGAL MALPRACTICE: A REMEDY WITHOUT REASON

Those who file malpractice suits against their lawyers usually find that the effort wasn't worth it, as evidenced by some alarming statistics recently released by the American Bar Association:

- Fewer than 30% of all malpractice claims filed against lawyers between 1983 and 1985 led to lawsuits—the rest were dismissed by state disciplinary boards as "inappropriate" after only a cursory look.

- Clients received no compensation in more than 63% of the lawsuits.

- Extremely few clients won more than $1,000.

- Clients who don't settle out of court win only 1.2% of the time.

38 Mediate Neighborhood Disputes

The claims that neighbors are less than neighborly run the gamut: They are loud. They refuse to pitch in to repair the fence on the lot line. Their kids are dangerous little monsters who menace others. The legal system—expensive, slow and adversarial—is ill-equipped to resolve these disputes.

Lawyers equate law with their own profit. Because fights between corporations or wealthy individuals generate plenty of billable hours, they are welcome in the formal legal system. But because ordinary folk can't afford lawyers' fees, there is no room in the courthouse for their arguments.

Most neighbor disputes, no matter how acrimonious, are defined by the legal system as "not legal"—a definition that conveniently allows them to be ignored. So too often these disputes fester, dividing the neighborhood and sometimes producing violence. Police and social agencies must cope as best they can with the unhappy result.

Arguing neighbors would have the chance to get a fair, fast and satisfying result if their disputes were resolved out of court, in mediation. Mediation is an informal way of settling disputes. People who have a complaint they wish to resolve meet with a trained mediator and attempt to negotiate a compromise that satisfies both sides.

The mediator acts mostly as a moderator, making sure each side gets a chance to speak up and helping both to define the dispute and arrive at an acceptable solution. Other than that, there are no complicated procedural rules, no transcript, no court schedules, no judges, no lawyers. If the parties need more time to hammer out a resolution, they can schedule more meetings. And if mediation fails, both sides are free to file a lawsuit.

Mediation is an especially good way to resolve many neighborhood disputes because it prevents them from escalating. Instead, fighting neighbors—who, after all, have an interest in getting along—are encouraged to talk civilly with one another, to work out a compromise together. Not only is their settlement apt to be more pleasing than one dictated by the court system, but they can reach it in private. They also save themselves from the intimidation and expense of the lawyer-controlled dog and pony show that masquerades as the legal system.

Mediation is not a new idea, but it is a relatively young one. The number of community mediation programs and mediators is burgeoning. A decade ago, there were 100 programs and 5,000 mediators nationwide; by 1990, there were 400 programs in 47 states and over 22,000 mediators.

And they get results. Mediation services report a settlement rate of between 80 and 90% of all cases.

Unfortunately, the majority of Americans are still denied access to community-based mediation programs. Some states and cities do a good job—in others, no programs exist or those that do are poorly publicized. In some places, the system has been too heavily infiltrated by lawyers, who tend to hinder rather than help by pitting the two sides against one another, turning negotiations into arguments.

WHAT TO DO

Mediation must be embraced as a preferred method for settling neighborhood disputes. Local community-based programs should offer free or reasonably-priced mediation.

Strong links should be maintained with small claims courts. Before neighbor disputes go to court, they should be evaluated with the idea of diverting as many of them as possible to mediation.

Mandatory training for mediators should emphasize the skills necessary to help disputants reach a compromise. Judges and lawyers schooled in the adversarial dispute resolution techniques of the courtroom need rigorous screening and retraining before becoming mediatiors.

Finally, mediated solutions should be as binding as any court judgment, eliminating the need to take the whole dispute to court if one party later backs out of the agreement.

IT'S HOW YOU PLAY THE GAME . . .

When his pleas for quiet fell on deaf ears, Michael Rubin turned his garden hose on his Los Angeles neighbor. The spray brought an abrupt end to Kenneth Schild's noisy game of basketball. But Schild retaliated by challenging Rubin in a court of law, where he won an order restraining Rubin from further harassment. Schild also claimed that the emotional harm from the hosing required him to seek psychiatric treatment.

Rubin responded with his own lawsuit—charging that his neighbor's persistent game of hoops not only deprived him of late afternoon naps, but caused him extreme mental anguish and devalued his home by at least $250,000.

Both Rubin and Schild are attorneys.

"What we have here," observed L.A. Superior Court Judge Marvin D. Rowen, "are lawyers utilizing their unlimited resources to accelerate a petty neighborhood squabble into a community war." Rowen ordered the lawyers to settle out of court—or he would throw them both in jail.

RESOURCES

To find a mediation program or a trained private mediator, contact:

American Bar Association

Standing Committee on Dispute Resolution

1800 M Street, NW

Washington, DC 20036

39 **Require Lawyer Impact Statements**

Japan produces engineers to "make the pie bigger," observed former Harvard University President Derek Bok, while America produces lawyers to divide the pie into smaller pieces. The more lawyers our society supports, the more litigious we become. Yet courts and legislatures unthinkingly and unceasingly produce laws that encourage lawyers to flourish.

Lawyers, through their domination of courts and legislatures, seem infinitely able to mandate measures that require the services of still more lawyers. It is not uncommon to hear lawyers say, only half tongue-in-cheek, that a particular court decision or statute is a "lawyers' full employment act." They mean that many issues are left to fight about in court—or that such complicated procedures have been set up that people will be forced to hire lawyers to help them through the maze.

This problem threatens to get worse as societal change creates whole new branches of the law, each producing work for many thousands of lawyers. There are several recent well-publicized examples.

- employment law: issues involving wrongful termination and injuries caused on the job by environmental hazards such as asbestos;
- health law: issues raised by terminating life support, surrogate pregnancies and notice requirements for abortions; and
- high tech law: issues relating to computer software and genetic engineering.

Long-existing legal areas have also been expanded, as courts have increased the number of theories that make a person legally liable for someone else's personal injury. For instance, in the early days of our country, a burglar couldn't sue a landowner for injuries suffered from a fall through a rotten roof while breaking in to steal. Under current theories of liability, however, the burglar might bring and win such a lawsuit.

Like the courts, legislatures also guarantee lots of litigation by creating new rights and remedies that depend on courts for their enforcement. For instance, Congress recently passed a law prohibiting workplace discrimination against the handicapped. While this law appropriately addresses some dreadful wrongs, enforcing it will create a lot of new work for lawyers.

Legislatures also create new work for lawyers by passing along irreconcilable differences between legislators and special interest groups to the courts in the form of ambiguous statutes. For example, suppose legislators can't agree on whether a new law should benefit all people who are living together as a family or only those who are married or related by blood. The warring factions may solve this impasse by using the word family—but not defining it. Hammering out the definition is left to the courts and the lawyers. Obviously, the more ambiguities legislation contains, the more lawyers needed to resolve them.

WHAT TO DO

A good start in getting control of the lawyer glut would be to require legislatures and appeals court judges to issue a public Lawyer Impact Statement for each case or proposed new law.

This is the same general approach that is used to identify adverse environmental effects that might result from proposed development project. For most of our history, land developers could go forward with no thought to environmental consequences of their actions. Then, the National Environmental Protection Act was passed by Congress in 1969. This law requires developers to assess and disclose, in an Environmental Impact Statement, how their proposed developments will affect the environment and why feasible alternatives that would have a less negative impact were not adopted.

Similarly, the Lawyer Impact Statement would:

- reveal if a statute or court decision is likely to create more work for lawyers because it uses ambiguous terms or creates a new right or benefit that depends on lawyers to enforce.
- identify possible alternatives that would require fewer lawyers—such as requiring mediation in case of a dispute, or clearly defining possible remedies.
- explain why the fewer-lawyer alternatives weren't adopted.

Mandatory Lawyer Impact Statements would force legislatures and courts to publicly acknowledge when their activities are contributing to the lawyer glut. The Statements would also provide groups that want to control the growth of lawyers in our society the means to target the worst lawyer-growth offenders for recall or defeat at the ballot box.

A MODEL SOLUTION

Lawyer Impact Statements could be modeled after the Fiscal Impact Statements now used by several state legislatures to keep track of how big a bite each new law may take out of the state budget. Here's how they work.

Each bill to be introduced in the legislature is assessed for its possible fiscal impact on the state. If a bill requires an appropriation, risks a substantial expenditure of state funds, or might cause a substantial decrease in state revenues, it is referred to the legislature's Fiscal Committee for further study. There, a detailed dollars-and-cents analysis is made for the legislators who will ultimately vote on the bill.

The Fiscal Committee also studies the bill's potential impact on city and county budgets. If the bill requires local expenditures, it must either provide for them or expressly disclaim state responsibility for raising the funds.

Fiscal consequences identified don't by themselves kill a law, but there is at least some public accountability—and interested citizens and activists are given the information they need to assess projects intelligently.

Ideas won't keep.

—Alfred North Whitehead
English philosopher

40 Create a National Idea Registry

Many of us produce at least one original idea in our lifetimes—an idea that could vastly improve the quality of many people's lives. But the laws controlling trade secrets, patents and copyrights are usually insufficient to encourage development of these ideas. The legal system treats most ideas, even great ones, as if they have no value.

Ideas are mysterious things. A wonderful plot for a novel, a brilliant product name, or a new way to open a can of peas can pop into our heads fully formed. Nothing is quite as exciting as the belief that we have produced something genuinely original.

Once the initial excitement wanes a little, our thoughts may turn to sharing the ideas with others—and possibly to fortune or at least public recognition of our brilliance.

Academic and scientific circles maintain elaborate systems for publishing original ideas and crediting their creators. Rewards come in the form of enhanced academic status and acceptance into the world of prestigious conferences and the potentially lucrative lecture circuit.

But this system rewards originality for a select few; most of us are cut out of the action. The only other outlet for good ideas is the marketplace. This is where our poor system of legal protection for ideas hurts us; it doesn't cultivate our collective creative genius.

Patent application procedures are so tortured that most people need legal assistance, which costs at least $2,000 to $4,000.

Thousands more in legal costs will likely be required to enforce the patent if someone infringes it.

Trade secrets usually benefit only their large business owners who use the economies of scale to exploit confidential information commerically. The individuals who come up with the ideas are seldom given credit, and have usually signed agreements giving the employer commercial rights over their efforts.

Copyright is sometimes thought to protect ideas. But it doesn't. Copyrights provide legal protection for the way ideas are expressed, not the ideas themselves. Of course, the first person to publish original ideas often benefits in the marketplace, but most good ideas very soon are taken over by hoards of less creative authors, composers and artists who come after.

The result is that of the millions of original ideas that flash into the world every day, only a relative few are developed into inventions or published in works protected by copyright. The rest are kept secret or lost to the public because the originator has no incentive to develop or disseminate them.

WHAT TO DO

As a society, we need to preserve and develop every good idea people come up with. To accomplish this, we should treat ideas as a national resource and create a National Idea Registry to record and encourage them. It could be operated by a public nonprofit corporation. Anyone could submit any idea along with a reasonable registration fee. Each idea would be date-stamped and assigned to an examiner who was an information and research specialist.

Recognizing that some ideas are simply too bizarre to be understood by anyone other than their creator, the examiner would first screen the idea for comprehensability. If the idea passed this test, the examiner would determine whether it had been publicly expressed in modern times—as just an idea, as an invention or in an artistic or literary expression.

If an idea were determined to be original, the creator would receive an Original Idea Certificate, and the idea would be entered in a computerized database and be made available to the public at nominal cost. An inventor, author or business could use registered ideas without charge.

The Registry would reward the creator in several ways. First, the creator could use the fact of registration as a convenient way to claim authorship if the idea turned out to be important. Second, to help good ideas become known, the Registry could publish a quarterly journal featuring the best ideas received. The Registry could also award prizes to the creators of particularly promising ideas.

Like nonprofit foundations that award grants and scholarships, the Registry would have broad discretion to decide what qualified as an original idea and which ideas were rewarded or recognized. Its decisions would be final.

If the Registry listed as original some ideas that weren't, anyone could submit a 100-word statement pointing out the mistake. If convinced of its error, the Registry would enter the statement in the database.

The Idea Registry would not replace the patent, copyright and trade secret approaches. An idea examiner who felt that an idea had potential for development as an invention or use as a trade secret would give the creator an opportunity to withdraw and develop it under one of these more traditional forms of idea protection.

COMPUTER BULLETIN BOARDS

Electronic bulletin boards are a relatively new forum for sharing ideas. All you need is a computer and modem; most bulletin boards are free or charge only a nominal fee. To participate in a forum—called a conference—you call the bulletin board through a modem, select from a menu the conference that you are interested in and select a topic. All bulletin boards provide instructions for users, and most are very easy to follow.

You can scan the contributions made by others, and if you want to jump in, you can type a comment or transmit one you've already prepared. Your contribution will appear for all to read. You can also have electronic dialogues—for days, weeks and even months—with other contributors.

Computer newsletters, magazines and stores all have information about bulletin boards.

CATALOG

ESTATE PLANNING & PROBATE

Plan Your Estate With a Living Trust
Attorney Denis Clifford
National 1st Edition
This book covers every significant aspect of estate planning and gives detailed specific, instructions for preparing a living trust, a document that lets your family avoid expensive and lengthy probate court proceedings after your death. *Plan Your Estate* includes all the tear-out forms and step-by-step instructions to let you prepare an estate plan designed for your special needs.
$19.95/NEST

Nolo's Simple Will Book
Attorney Denis Clifford
National 2nd Edition
It's easy to write a legally valid will using this book. The instructions and forms enable people to draft a will for all needs, including naming a personal guardian for minor children, leaving property to minor children or young adults and updating a will when necessary. Good in all states except Louisiana.
$17.95/SWIL

The Power of Attorney Book
Attorney Denis Clifford
National 4th Edition
Who will take care of your affairs, and make your financial and medical decisions if you can't? With this book you can appoint someone you trust to carry out your wishes and stipulate exactly what kind of care you want or don't want. Includes Durable Power of Attorney and Living Will Forms.
$19.95/POA

How to Probate an Estate
Julia Nissley
California 6th Edition
If you find yourself responsible for winding up the legal and financial affairs of a deceased family member or friend, you can often save costly attorneys' fees by handling the probate process yourself. This book shows you the simple procedures you can use to transfer assets that don't require probate, including property held in joint tenancy or living trusts or as community property.
$34.95/PAE

The Conservatorship Book
Lisa Goldoftas & Attorney Carolyn Farren
California 1st Edition
When a family member or close relative becomes incapacitated due to illness or age, it may be necessary to name a conservator for taking charge of their medical and financial affairs. *The Conservatorship Book* will help you determine when and what kind of conservatorship is necessary. The book comes with complete instructions and all the forms necessary to file a conservatorship.
$24.95/CON

GOING TO COURT

Everybody's Guide to Small Claims Court
Attorney Ralph Warner
National 5th Edition
California 9th Edition
These books will help you decide if you should sue in small claims court, show you how to file and serve papers, tell you what to bring to court and how to collect a judgment.
National $15.95/NSCC
California $14.95/ CSCC

Fight Your Ticket

Attorney David Brown
California 4th Edition
This book shows you how to fight an unfair traffic ticket—when you're stopped, at arraignment, at trial and on appeal.
$17.95/FYT

The Criminal Records Book

Attorney Warren Siegel
California 3rd Edition
This book shows you step-by-step how to seal criminal records, dismiss convictions, destroy marijuana records and reduce felony convictions.
$19.95/CRIM

Collect Your Court Judgment

Gini Graham Scott, Attorney
Stephen Elias &
Lisa Goldoftas
California 2nd Edition
This book contains step-by-step instructions and all the forms you need to collect a court judgment from the debtor's bank accounts, wages, business receipts, real estate or other assets.
$19.95/JUDG

How to Change Your Name

Attorneys David Loeb & David Brown
California 5th Edition
This book explains how to change your name legally and provides all the necessary court forms with detailed instructions on how to fill them out.
$19.95/NAME

LEGAL REFORM

Legal Breakdown: 40 Ways to Fix Our Legal System

Nolo Press Editors and Staff
National 1st Edition
Legal Breakdown presents 40 common sense proposals to make our legal system fairer, faster, cheaper and more accessible. It explains such things as why we should abolish probate, take divorce out of court, treat jurors better and give them more power, and make a host of other fundamental changes.
$8.95/LEG

MONEY MATTERS

Barbara Kaufman'sConsumer Action Guide

Barbara Kaufman
California 1st Edition
This practical handbook is filled with information on hundreds of consumer topics. Barbara Kaufman, the Bay Area's award-winning host and producer of KCBS Radio's *Call for Action*, gives consumers access to their legal rights, providing addresses and phone numbers of where to complain where things to wrong, and providing resources if more help is necessary.
$14.95/CAG

Money Troubles: Legal Strategies to Cope With Your Debts

Attorney Robin Leonard
National 1st Edition
Are you behind on your credit card bills or loan payments? If you are, then *Money Troubles* is exactly what you need. Covering everything from knowing what your rights are—and asserting them to helping you evaluate your individual situation, this practical, straightforward book is for anyone who needs help understanding and dealing with the complex and often scary topic of debts.
$16.95/MT

How to File for Bankruptcy

Attorneys Stephen Elias, Albin Renauer & Robin Leonard
National 3rd Edition
Trying to decide whether or not filing for bankruptcy makes sense? *How to File for Bankruptcy* contains an overview of the process and all the forms plus step-by-step instructions on the procedures to follow.
$24.95/HFB

Simple Contracts for Personal Use

Attorney Stephen Elias
National 2nd Edition
This book contains clearly written legal form contracts to buy and sell property, borrow and lend money, store and lend personal property, release others from personal liability, or pay a contractor to do home repairs.
$16.95/CONT

FAMILY MATTERS

The Living Together Kit
Attorneys Toni Ihara & Ralph Warner
National 6th Edition
The Living Together Kit is a detailed guide designed to help the increasing number of unmarried couples living together understand the laws that affect them. Sample agreements and instructions are included.
$17.95/LTK

A Legal Guide for Lesbian and Gay Couples
Attorneys Hayden Curry & Denis Clifford
National 6th Edition
Laws designed to regulate and protect unmarried couples don't apply to lesbian and gay couples. This book shows you step-by-step how to write a living-together contract, plan for medical emergencies, and plan your estates. Includes forms, sample agreements and lists of both national lesbian and gay legal organizations, and AIDS organizations.
$17.95/LG

The Guardianship Book
Lisa Goldoftas & Attorney David Brown
California 1st Edition
The Guardianship Book provides step-by-step instructions and the forms needed to obtain a legal guardianship without a lawyer.
$19.95/GB

How to Do Your Own Divorce
Attorney Charles Sherman
(Texas Ed. by Sherman & Simons)
California 17th Edition & Texas 2nd Edition
These books contain all the forms and instructions you need to do your divorce without a lawyer.
California $18.95/CDIV
Texas $14.95/TDIV

Practical Divorce Solutions
Attorney Charles Sherman
California 2nd Edition
This book is a valuable guide to the emotional aspects of divorce as well as an overview of the legal and financial decisions that must be made.
$12.95/PDS

How to Adopt Your Stepchild in California
Frank Zagone & Attorney Mary Randolph
California 3rd Edition
There are many emotional, financial and legal reasons to adopt a stepchild, but among the most pressing legal reasons is the need to avoid confusion over inheritance or guardianship. This book provides sample forms and step-by-step instructions for completing a simple uncontested adoption by a stepparent
$19.95/ADOP

California Marriage & Divorce Law
Attorneys Ralph Warner, Toni Ihara & Stephen Elias
California 11th Edition
This book explains community property, pre-nuptial contracts, foreign marriages, buying a house, getting a divorce, dividing property, and more.
$19.95/MARR

PATENT, COPYRIGHT & TRADEMARK

Patent It Yourself
Attorney David Pressman
National 3rdEdition
From the patent search to the actual application, this book covers everything from use and licensing, successful marketing and how to deal with infringement.
$34.95/PAT

The Inventor's Notebook
Fred Grissom & Attorney David Pressman
National 1st Edition
This book helps you document the process of successful independent inventing by providing forms, instructions, references to relevant areas of patent law, a bibliography of legal and non-legal aids and more.
$19.95/INOT

How to Copyright Software
Attorney M.J. Salone
National 3rd Edition
This book tells you how to register your copyright for maximum protection and discusses who owns a copyright on software developed by more than one person.
$39.95/COPY

BUSINESS

How to Write a Business Plan
Mike McKeever
National 3rd Edition
If you're thinking of starting a business or raising money to expand an existing one, this book will show you how to write the business plan and loan package necessary to finance your business and make it work.
$17.95/SBS

Marketing Without Advertising
Michael Phillips & Salli Rasberry
National 1st Edition
This book outlines practical steps for building and expanding a small business without spending a lot of money on advertising.
$14.00/MWA

The Partnership Book
Attorneys Denis Clifford & Ralph Warner
National 4th Edition
This book shows you step-by-step how to write a solid partnership agreement that meets your needs. It covers initial contributions to the business, wages, profit-sharing, buy-outs, death or retirement of a partner and disputes.
$24.95/PART

How to Form Your Own Nonprofit Corporation
Attorney Anthony Mancuso
National 1st Edition
This book explains the legal formalities involved and provides detailed information on the differences in the law among 50 states. It also contains forms for the Articles, Bylaws and Minutes you need, along with complete instructions for obtaining federal 501 (c) (3) tax exemptions and qualifying for public charity status.
$24.95/NNP

The California Nonprofit Corporation Handbook
Attorney Anthony Mancuso
California 6th Edition
This book shows you step-by-step how to form and operate a nonprofit corporation in California. It includes the latest corporate and tax law changes, and the forms for the Articles, Bylaws and Minutes.
$29.95/NON

How to Form Your Own Corporation
Attorney Anthony Mancuso
California 7th Edition
New York 2nd Edition
Florida 3rd Edition
These books contain the forms, instructions and tax information you need to incorporate a small business yourself and save hundreds of dollars in lawyers' fees.
California $29.95/CCOR
New York $24.95/NYCO
Florida $24.95/FLCO

The California Professional Corporation Handbook
Attorney Anthony Mancuso
California 4th Edition
Health care professionals, lawyers, accountants and members of certain other professions must fulfill special requirements when forming a corporation in California. This book contains up-to-date tax information plus all the forms and instructions necessary to form a California professional corporation.
$34.95/PROF

The Independent Paralegal's Handbook
Attorney Ralph Warner
National 2nd Edition
The Independent Paralegal's Handbook provides legal and business guidelines for those who want to take routine legal work out of the law office and offer it for a reasonable fee in an independent business.
$19.95/ PARA

Getting Started as an Independent Paralegal
(Two Audio Tapes)
Attorney Ralph Warner
National 1st Edition
Approximately three hours in all, these tapes are a carefully edited version of a seminar given by Nolo Press founder Ralph Warner. They are designed to be used with *The Independent Paralegal's Handbook.*
$24.95/GSIP

HOMEOWNERS

How to Buy a House in California
Attorney Ralph Warner, Ira Serkes & George Devine
California 1st Edition
This book shows you how to find a house, work with a real estate agent, make an offer and negotiate intelligently. Includes information on all types of mortgages as well as private financing options.
$18.95/BHC

For Sale By Owner
George Devine
California 1st Edition
For Sale By Owner provides essential information about pricing your house, marketing it, writing a contract and going through escrow.
$24.95/FSBO

The Deeds Book
Attorney Mary Randolph
California 1st Edition
If you own real estate, you'll need to sign a new deed when you transfer the property or put it in trust as part of your estate planning. This book shows you how
$15.95/DEED

Homestead Your House
Attorneys Ralph Warner, Charles Sherman & Toni Ihara
California 7th Edition
This book shows you how to file a Declaration of Homestead and includes complete instructions and tear-out forms.
$9.95/HOME

LANDLORDS & TENANTS

The Landlord's Law Book: Rights & Responsibilities
Attorneys David Brown & Ralph Warner
California 3rd Edition
This book contains information on deposits, leases and rental agreements, inspections (tenant's privacy rights), habitability (rent withholding), ending a tenancy, liability and rent control.
$29.95/LBRT

The Landlord's Law Book: Evictions
Attorney David Brown
California 3rd Edition
Updated for 1991, this book will show you step-by-step how to go to court and get an eviction for a tenant who won't pay rent—and won't leave. Contains all the tear-out forms and necessary instructions.
$29.95/LBEV

Tenant's Rights
Attorneys Myron Moskovitz & Ralph Warner
California 11th Edition
This book explains the best way to handle your relationship both your landlord and your legal rights when you find yourself in disagreement. A special section on rent control cities is included.
$15.95/CTEN

OLDER AMERICANS

Elder Care: Choosing & Financing Long-Term Care
Attorney Joseph Matthews
National 1st Edition
This book will guide you in choosing and paying for long-term care, alerting you to practical concerns and explaining laws that may affect your decisions.
$16.95/ELD

Social Security, Medicare & Pensions

Attorney Joseph Matthews with Dorothy Matthews Berman
National 5th Edition
This book contains invaluable guidance through the current maze of rights and benefits for those 55 and over, including Medicare, Medicaid and Social Security retirement and disability benefits and age discrimination protections.
$15.95/SOA

JUST FOR FUN

29 Reasons Not to Go to Law School

Attorneys Ralph Warner & Toni Ihara
National 3rd Edition
Filled with humor and piercing observations, this book can save you three years, $70,000 and your sanity.
$9.95/29R

Devil's Advocates: The Unnatural History of Lawyers

by Andrew & Jonathan Roth
National 1st Edition
This book is a painless and hilarious education, tracing the legal profession. Careful attention is given to the world's worst lawyers, most preposterous cases and most ludicrous courtroom strategies.
$12.95/DA

Poetic Justice: The Funniest, Meanest Things Ever Said About Lawyers

Edited by Jonathan & Andrew Roth
National 1st Edition
A great gift for anyone in the legal profession who has managed to maintain a sense of humor.
$8.95/PJ

RESEARCH & REFERENCE

Legal Research

Attorney Stephen Elias
National 2nd Edition
A valuable tool on its own or as a companion to just about every other Nolo book. This book gives easy-to-use, step-by-step instructions on how to find legal information.
$14.95/LRES

Family Law Dictionary

Attorneys Robin Leonard & Stephen Elias
National 2nd Edition
Finally, a legal dictionary that's written in plain English, not "legalese"! *The Family Law Dictionary* is designed to help the nonlawyer who has a question or problem involving family law—marriage, divorce, adoption or living together.
$13.95/FLD

A Dictionary of Patent, Copyright & Trademark Terms

Attorney Stephen Elias
National 2nd Edition
This book explains the terms associated with trade secrets, copyrights, trademarks, patents and contracts.
$15.95/IPLD

Legal Research Made Easy: A Roadmap Through the Law Library Maze

2-1/2 hr. videotape and 40-page manual
Nolo Press/Legal Star Communications
If you're a law student, paralegal or librarian—or just want to look up the law for yourself—this video is for you. University of California law professor Bob Berring explains how to use all the basic legal research tools in your local law library.
$89.95/LRME

THE NEIGHBORHOOD

Dog Law

Attorney Mary Randolph
National 1st Edition
Dog Law is a practical guide to the laws that affect dog owners and their neighbors. You'll find answers to common questions on such topics as biting, barking, veterinarians and more.
$12.95/DOG

Neighbor Law: Fences, Trees, Boundaries & Noise

Attorney Cora Jordan
National 1st Edition
Neighbor Law answers common questions about the subjects that most often trigger disputes between neighbors. It explains how to find the law and resolve disputes without a nasty lawsuit.
$14.95 NEI

SOFTWARE

WillMaker

Nolo Press/Legisoft
National 4th Edition
This easy-to-use software program lets you prepare and update a legal will—safely, privately and without the expense of a lawyer. Leading you step-by-step in a question-and-answer format, *WillMaker* builds a will around your answers, taking into account your state of residence. *WillMaker* comes with a 200-page legal manual which provides the legal background necessary to make sound choices. Good in all states except Louisiana.
IBM PC
(3-1/2 & 5-1/4 disks included)
$69.95/WI4
MACINTOSH $69.95/WM4

For the Record

Carol Pladsen & Attorney Ralph Warner
National 2nd Edition
For the Record program provides a single place to keep a complete inventory of all your important legal, financial, personal and family records. It can compute your net worth and also create inventories of all insured property to protect your assets in the event of fire or theft. Includes a 200-page manual filled with practical and legal advice.
IBM PC
(3-1/2 & 5-1/4 disks included)
$59.95/FRI2
MACINTOSH $59.95/FRM2

California Incorporator

Attorney Anthony Mancuso/Legisoft
California 1st Edition
Answer the questions on the screen and this software program will print out the 35-40 pages of documents you need to make your California corporation legal. Comes with a 200-page manual which explains the incorporation process.
IBM PC
(3-1/2 & 5-1/4 disks included)
$129.00/INCI

How to Form Your Own New York Corporation & How to Form Your Own Texas Corporation

Computer Editions
Attorney Anthony Mancuso
These book/software packages contain the instructions and tax information and forms you need to incorporate a small business and save hundreds of dollars in lawyers' fees. All organizational forms are on disk. Both come with a 250-page manual.

New York 1st Edition
IBM PC 5-1/4 $69.95/NYCI
IBM PC 3-1/2 $69.95/NYC3I
MACINTOSH $69.95/NYCM

Texas 1st Edition
IBM PC 5-1/4 $69.95/TCI
IBM PC 3-1/2 $69.95/TC3I
MACINTOSH $69.95/TCM

The California Nonprofit Corporation Handbook

(computer edition)
Attorney Anthony Mancuso
California 1st Edition
This book/software package shows you step-by-step how to form and operate a nonprofit corporation in California. Included on disk are the forms for the Articles, Bylaws and Minutes.
IBM PC 5-1/4 $69.95/NPI
IBM PC 3-1/2 $69.95/NP3I
MACINTOSH $69.95/NPM

VISIT OUR STORE

If you live in the Bay Area, be sure to visit the Nolo Press Bookstore on the corner of 9th & Parker Streets in West Berkeley. You'll find our complete line of books and software—new and "damaged"—all at a discount. We also have t-shirts, posters and a selection of business and legal self-help books from other publishers.

Hours

Monday to Friday	10 a.m. to 5 p.m.
Thursdays	Until 6 p.m
Saturdays	10 a.m. to 4:30 p.m.
Sundays	10 a.m. to 3 p.m.

950 Parker Street, Berkeley, California

ORDER FORM

Name

Address (UPS to street address, Priority Mail to P.O. boxes)

Catalog Code	Quantity	Item	Unit price	Total
		Subtotal		
		Sales tax (California residents only)		
		Shipping & handling		
		2nd day UPS		
		TOTAL		

SALES TAX
California residents add your local tax:
7 1/4%, 7 3/4%, or 8 1/4%

SHIPPING & HANDLING
$4.00   1 item
$5.00   2-3 items
+$.50   each additional item
Allow 2-3 weeks for delivery

IN A HURRY?
UPS 2nd day delivery is available:
Add $5.00 (contiguous states) or
$8.00 (Alaska & Hawaii) to your regular shipping and handling charges

PRICES SUBJECT TO CHANGE

FOR FASTER SERVICE, USE YOUR CREDIT CARD AND OUR TOLL-FREE NUMBERS:
Monday-Friday, 7 a.m. to 5 p.m. Pacific Time

US	1 (800) 992-6656
CA (outside 510 area code)	1 (800) 640-6656
(inside 510 area code)	549-1976
General Information	1 (510) 549-1976
Fax us your order	1 (510) 548-5902

METHOD OF PAYMENT
☐ Check enclosed
☐ VISA   ☐ Mastercard   ☐ Discover Card
☐ American Expess

Account #   Expiration Date

Signature

Phone

LEG

NOLO PRESS / 950 PARKER STREET / BERKELEY CA 94710

Keep Up To Date With the *Nolo News*

Nolo Press publishes a complete line of self-help law books and software programs—they are affordable, they explain (in plain English) what the law says, and they show readers how to handle many routine tasks without a lawyer.

Nolo also publishes a quarterly newspaper, the *Nolo News*. It contains an update section to keep readers up-to-date on law changes that affect our books, and explores legal issues of interest to non-lawyers. In addition, the *Nolo News* contains book reviews, an ever-popular lawyer joke column, and a complete catalog of Nolo products.

Send in the registration card below and receive a FREE two-year subscription to the *Nolo News* (normally $12). Your subscription will begin with the first issue published after we receive your card.

N O L O

BUSINESS REPLY MAIL

FIRST-CLASS MAIL PERMIT NO 3283 BERKELEY CA

POSTAGE WILL BE PAID BY ADDRESSEE

NOLO PRESS
950 Parker Street
Berkeley CA 94710-9867

NO POSTAGE
NECESSARY
IF MAILED
IN THE
UNITED STATES